ISRAEL:
VOICES
FROM
WITHIN

Israel: Voices From Within

Edited by

Barry Chazan

Shai Chazan

Yehudit Werchow

Published by

Third Place Publications

Third Place Publications
95 Revere Drive, Suite D
Northbrook, IL 60062

Cover Image: Shira Stav
Cover Design: Kristy Scher
Layout: Meredith Swartz

ISBN: 978-1-7350808-0-2
Printed in the United States of America
First Printing, May 2020

For accompanying materials and resources, visit:
theicenter.org/voicesfromwithin

"A child is something else..."

Yehuda Amichai

Table of Contents

NOTE ON TITLES: Several of the poems in this volume do not have titles. The first line of the poem is used as the title in the table of contents and appears in brackets — [At the window she sits...] — when there is none. On the page where the poem appears, in lieu of a title the first line will be used in quotation marks followed by an ellipsis — "At the window she sits..." — as is the convention. For certain poems, an asterisk will act in lieu of a title, as per specific contractual agreements.

NOTE ON POET'S NAMES: The names of the poets in this volume are all transliterated from Russian, German, Yiddish, Polish, Arabic, and Hebrew into English. As many of the poets' names are inconsistently transliterated, this volume has elected to use the recognized transliterations of ACUM (the Israeli copyright administrator) and the Institute for the Translation of Hebrew Literature.

ISRAEL: VOICES FROM WITHIN

Introduction

What this
book is about

At its core, this is a book about Israel. It tells the story of Israel through the presentation of a collection of poems from the early 1900s until today. These poems reflect the personal thoughts and feelings of diverse poets about issues specifically related to Palestine and the newly created State of Israel, such as returning to an ancient home, working the land, and building a new society, along with reflections on issues related to all of human life, such as love, joy, sadness and meaning. Through the poets' myriad voices, you, the reader, are invited to engage with an array of viewpoints about statehood and homeland, religion and secularism, settlement and accommodation, and, above all else, the human condition.

While the story of Israel is at the core of this text, its subject is actually *you*. This book does not intend to talk *about* Israel, but rather to enable Israel to converse *with* you. It does not intend to preach to you, teach you, or beseech you; all it wants to do is talk with you. This book is about conversations between you and people who shaped the State of Israel and reflected on its everyday life through language. The voices with whom you will engage represent a unique group of individuals who expressed strikingly personal and enduringly collective feelings, ideas, and insights. They have penned these lines, from the dawn of modern Hebrew in the late 19th century until today, for *you* to read, reflect on, and discuss with *them*.

Some of these poems were written outside of Israel, in places like Odessa, Vilna, and Warsaw; some were written in pre-state Palestine; some were written during the era of the creation of the State; and many were written in our day and age.

We chose poetry as our story-telling medium as it is very much tied to the saga of Israel, past and present. The dream of a homeland for Jews was not only expressed in the language of politics; it was presented in poems, essays, manifestos, short stories, novels, and feuilletons. Indeed, many people regarded the act of writing poetry in Hebrew as a step on the path to national redemption. In writing verse in Hebrew, the poets were not merely attempting to compare beloveds "to a summer's day," but, in their way, they viewed it as the making of history. In tribute to these shapers of history, the streets and avenues of the State of Israel today carry the names of poets and authors alongside significant biblical and political leaders.

Poets in pre- and post-state Israel were not isolated individuals writing in far-off dark rooms, but rather they were very often people who frequented cafés in Tel Aviv, whose poems were published in weekend newspapers, and who were consulted by presidents, prime ministers, and other political leaders. Our poets speak to the land, to its people, to us and indeed to each other as, in fact, many of the poems are actually conversing with each other. Perhaps, most significantly, many of the poems of pre- and post-state Israel became an important part of the popular songbook of Israeli life; heard on the radio and on television and regularly sung by schoolchildren and adults. Indeed, in many ways, poetry is one of the primary pathways to come to know Israel from "within." The poems in this volume present engaging portraits of personal landscapes and over-arching ideologies of people who dreamt about and built Israel and, at the same time, fell in and out of love, knew great sadness and delight, and performed the mundane task of shopping for their families against the cosmic backdrop of holy sites and memories.

Poetry can be daunting for readers. At the same time, it is a medium that invites very personal conversations and exchanges. In an effort to make Israel's poetic canon more accessible, the book's poems are organized into four sections, which are both chronological and thematic, presenting a wide collection of voices and visions of Israel. Each section begins with an introduction to the era, followed by a brief biographical summary of the poet. Following the biography, the poems are presented along with periodic annotations included to help you navigate the poem with relative ease. The purpose of the annotations is not to deprive you of the joy of finding your own explanations of the poet's ideas, but rather to explicate certain phrases, sources, and background information in order to facilitate your own personal experience and interpretation of the poems. This is the first book to utilize *The Hebrew Bible: a Translation with Commentary* by Robert Alter (New York, NY: W.W. Norton & Company, 2019), a historic new translation which will greatly enhance and enrich the remarkable connection between the majesty of biblical Hebrew and modern Hebrew poetry.

We hope this book provides you with a meaningful way of talking *with* Israel and not *about* Israel. Its primary aim is to give you an understanding of the country's many faces and voices; its personal howls and hallelujahs, and its collective sighs, smiles, and aspirations during this remarkable chapter in the history of human and Jewish life.

By Barry Chazan

ISRAEL: VOICES FROM WITHIN

Section 1

Early Voices
The View from Afar

The Zionist movement emerged from the confrontation between traditional Jewish life and modernity. It was one of several responses of the Jewish people to new forms of religiosity, nationalism, identity and emancipation. The new worldview known as Zionism was most presciently verbalized by the Hungarian-born journalist, Theodor Herzl, who is generally regarded as the founder of what is called the Zionist Movement. His political efforts led to the historic First Zionist Congress in 1897, in Basel, where the movement was formally established.

This late 19th century political thrust was paralleled and indeed preceded by a significant new cultural movement. In that era, poets, short story writers, essayists, and novelists in Europe and across large swaths of the Russian Empire were spearheading a campaign of literary revival. These writings reflected both general literary influences, as well as Jewish sources, terminologies, and references, and covered a broad range of topics related to the condition and the lives of Jews in those times. Many of these authors expressed a distancing from traditional religious life and an apparent affinity for prevailing general cultural styles and worldviews just as these same authors began to confront waves of anti-Jewish biases and prejudices, often accompanied by exclusionary and nationalistic worldviews. This dynamic of supposed emancipation alongside increasing anti-Jewish biases, led many Jewish cultural figures to begin to dream of a Jewish renaissance rooted in a Jewish-Hebrew land, language, and culture. The combination of developments in society at large along with political and cultural dynamics within Jewish communities sparked a new vision of renewal, an emancipation that sought to re-connect Jews to their ancient land—Israel—and to their ancient language—Hebrew.

Many of the pre-state Hebrew poets, novelists, and essayists were not born in the Land of Israel *(Eretz Yisrael)* nor had they seen it. Nevertheless, they mused, dreamed, and fantasized about The Land of Israel—often influenced by biblical terms and descriptions about the hope and nature of "returning to Zion"—or a new Jewish homeland.

Chaim Nachman Bialik, Shaul Tchernichovsky, and Rachel Bluwstein (known as Rahel or Rahel the Poet) are frequently regarded as exemplary voices of early 20th-century Zionist writing and are among the founding voices of modern Hebrew poetry. Their verse is redolent with the influence of traditional Jewish culture and at the same time glows with the emergent Hebraism of the early 20th century. This poetry also contains a distinctly Slavic poetic sensibility and mirrors prominent Russian writers of the time. Their writings reflect the transition from the old world to the new, charting the struggles and triumphs that accompanied a clear-eyed and poetic yearning.

Daniel Gordis, *Israel: a Concise History of a Nation Reborn* (New York: Ecco Books, 2016), 15-66.

Anita Shapira, *Israel: A History* (Waltham, Mass.: Brandeis University Press, 2012), 3-26.

Gil Troy, *The Zionist Ideas: Visions for the Jewish Homeland Then, Now, Tomorrow* (Philadelphia: The Jewish Publication Society, 2018), 3-139.

Chaim Nachman Bialik

(1873–1934)

Chaim Nachman Bialik was born in the town of Radi in the Ukraine. He lived most of his early years with his pious grandfather in Zhitomir, and from 1890-1891 he studied at the religious yeshiva in Volozhin. Subsequently, he lived mainly in Odessa and then settled in Israel, where he was grandly and graciously received in 1924. He died ten years later and is buried in the Trumpeldor Cemetery in Tel Aviv.

Bialik's poetry was influenced by classical Jewish texts, medieval Hebrew poetry, *Haskalah*-inspired Hebrew *belles lettres*, and prominent Jewish events in his lifetime, as well as by the works of Western and Eastern European poets and writers. Bialik was denoted alternatively as Israel's "national poet," "the poet laureate of the Jewish people," and the "Poet of the Renaissance of the Jewish people." His writings reflect a (sometimes nostalgic) metamorphosis from the great texts—embracing piety, perpetual communal suffering, and ultimate powerlessness of traditional Jewish life—to a vision of empowerment and the dream of a new Jewish homeland. In addition, he is often regarded as having played a significant role in the introduction of a "secular Judaism" to the public sphere of pre-state life in Palestine.

BACKGROUND:

Avner Holtzman, *Hayim Nachman Bialik* (New Haven: Yale University Press, 2017).

Gordis, *Israel: A Concise History of a Nation Reborn*, 11–16, 18–19.

Shapira, *Israel: A History*, 148–149.

Troy, *The Zionist Ideas*, 112–116.

From **"To the Bird"**

Welcome back, lovely bird,[1]
from hot lands to my window —
I died for your sweet song in winter,
after you left me at home.

Sing of miracles far away.
Is there, dear bird, tell me,
much evil there too, and pain
in that land of warmth, of beauty?

Do you sing greetings
from fruited valley and hill?
Has God pitied, comforted Zion,
or is she a graveyard still?[2]

Tears are done, hope is gone —[3]
but my torment has no end.
Welcome back, precious bird,
sing out your joyful song!

Spring 1891   *Translated by David Aberbach*

[1] The word *shuvah* means "return" and suggests both the religious concept of *teshuvah* (repentance) as well as the emergent turn-of-century movement *Shivat Zion* (Return to Zion), which pioneered emigration to Palestine. The bird is reminiscent of the dove in the biblical story of Noah: "And the dove came back to him at eventide and, look, a plucked olive leaf was in its bill, and Noah knew that the waters had abated from the earth." (Genesis 8:11)

[2] Over the centuries, the Land of Israel became a place to be buried rather than a place in which to live.

[3] While the tears of exile and longing are replaced by the joy of return, for some reason the poet declares his own personal torment to be endless.

אֶל הַצִּפּוֹר

שָׁלוֹם רָב שׁוּבֵךְ, צִפּוֹרָה נֶחְמֶדֶת,
מֵאַרְצוֹת הַחֹם אֶל־חַלּוֹנִי –
אֶל קוֹלֵךְ כִּי עָרֵב מַה־נַּפְשִׁי כָלָתָה
בַּחֹרֶף בְּעָזְבֵךְ מְעוֹנִי.

זַמְּרִי, סַפֵּרִי, צִפּוֹרִי הַיְקָרָה,
מֵאֶרֶץ מֶרְחַקִּים נִפְלָאוֹת,
הֲגַם שָׁם בָּאָרֶץ הַחַמָּה, הַיָּפָה,
תִּרְבֶּינָה הָרָעוֹת, הַתְּלָאוֹת?

הֲתִשְׂאִי לִי שָׁלוֹם מִזְמַרַת הָאָרֶץ,
מֵעֵמֶק, מִגַּיְא, מֵרֹאשׁ הָרִים?
הֲרַחַם, הֲנִחַם אֱלוֹהַּ אֶת־צִיּוֹן,
אִם עוֹדָהּ עֲזוּבָה לִקְבָרִים?

כִּכָּר בָּר כָּלוּ הַדְּמָעוֹת, כִּכָּר בָּר הַקָּצִים –
וְלֹא הֲקִיץ הַקֵּץ עַל יְגוֹנִי.
שָׁלוֹם רָב שׁוּבֵךְ, צִפּוֹרִי הַיְקָרָה,
צַהֲלִי־נָא קוֹלֵךְ וָרֹנִּי!

נִיסָן, תרנ"א.

"At the window she sits..."

At the window she sits
combing her hair,[1]
to you a whore —[2]
to me she's pure.

Bitter my heart,
bitter today,
if Rochele's gone —[3]
what can I say?

People have tongues
for gossip and worse,[4]
but Rochele's mine
and I hers.[5]

Bitter my heart...

At dusk I walk
the path through the corn
without Rochele—
my soul is shorn.

Bitter my heart...

Stalks and ears of corn:
tell Rochele I love her a lot.
Swear: if she's late
I'll die on the spot.

Bitter my heart...

Translated by David Aberbach

[1] According to some religious practices, married women cover their hair or wear wigs as a sign of modesty. The poem's protagonist is a new type of woman, one who sits by the window combing her hair and reflecting on love and loneliness.

[2] In lines 3 and 9-10, Bialik uses words related to debauchery and gossip to contrast with the purity of the poet's love.

[3] The woman's name is Rachel, but the poet uses the affectionate Yiddish diminutive, Rochele. The biblical Rachel was the wife of the patriarch Jacob and the mother of Joseph and Benjamin, two of his 12 sons. Rachel was probably the most inspirational of the matriarchs; she died during childbirth and appears throughout Jewish history as caring for her people: "Thus said the LORD: A voice in Ramah is heard, lament and bitter weeping..." (Jeremiah 31:14)

[4] While the word for "to gossip" is spelled differently from the name of the biblical Rachel or the Rochele of this poem, the words sound the same.

[5] "My lover is mine and I am his, who grazes among the lilies." (Song of Songs 2:16)

הִיא יוֹשְׁבָה לַחַלּוֹן

הִיא יוֹשְׁבָה לַחַלּוֹן
וְשׂוֹרְקָה שְׂעָרָהּ,
בְּעֵינֵיכֶם הִיא פְרוּצָה
וּבְעֵינַי הִיא בָרָה.

מַר לִי מָר, לִבִּי
הַיּוֹם עָלַי רָע,
אִם רָחֵלָה אֵינֶנָּה–
אֲנִי אָנָה בָא?

פֶּה יֵשׁ לַבְּרִיּוֹת
וְהוֹלְכוֹת הֵן רָכִיל,
אַךְ רָחֵלָה לִי הִיא
וְאָנֹכִי לְרָחֵל.

מַר לִי...

בָּעֶרֶב כִּי־אֵצֵא
אֶל מִשְׁעוֹל הַקָּמָה –
רָחֵלָה אֵין עִמִּי –
אֵין עִמִּי הַנְּשָׁמָה.

מַר לִי...

שִׁבֳּלִים, גִּבְעוֹלִים,
לְרָחֵלָה שְׂאוּ שְׁלוֹמִי
עֲנוּ בִי: אִם תְּאַחֵר –
מָתַי בִּמְקוֹמִי.

מַר לִי...

From **"Blessing of the Nation"**

Strengthen the hands[1] of our remarkable brethren[2]
Who reshape the dust of our land[3]
Let their spirit not fall but be exultant and joyful[4]
Let us come together—shoulder to shoulder—[5] for the salvation
of our nation![6]

Translated by Barry Chazan

This selection, from Bialik's longer poem of the same name, was written in 1894 during the first wave of Jewish immigration to Palestine (1882–1900) in response to a request for an anthem. These words were subsequently set to stirring music (apparently to a Russian folk song) and became one of the prominent songs of the Zionist movement, periodically suggested as the national anthem.

The poem's title in Hebrew—_birkat ha'am_—is a secularized version of traditional religious prayers such as the _birkat hamazon_ (Grace After Meals).

[1] "Will your heart stand the test, will your hands be strong, in the days I am about to set against you? I am the LORD. I have spoken and I have done." (Ezekiel 22:14)

[2] "Brethren" might suggest the language of the emergent socialist ethos, although Bialik himself was reputed to have rejected this interpretation.

[3] "Reshaping the dust of our land," refers to the custom of burying Jews from abroad in Palestine upon their death. The same phrase is now transformed into the creation of a flourishing and furrowed land of life and rebirth.

[4] "Let the field be glad and all that is in it, then shall all the trees of the forest gladly sing." (Psalms 96:12)

[5] "Shoulder to shoulder" might suggest a credo of shared labor for a common cause.

[6] The phrase "to the salvation of our nation" is a secular version of the traditional religious phrase "with God's help" (_b'ezrat haShem_).

בִּרְכַּת עָם

תֶּחֱזַקְנָה יְדֵי כָל־אַחֵינוּ הַמְחוֹנְנִים
עַפְרוֹת אַרְצֵנוּ בַּאֲשֶׁר הֵם שָׁם;
אַל יִפֹּל רוּחֲכֶם – עַלִּיזִים, מִתְרוֹנְנִים
בֹּאוּ שְׁכֶם אֶחָד לְעֶזְרַת הָעָם!

From **"In the City of Slaughter"**

Get up and go to the city of slaughter,[1]
see with your own eyes,
feel with your hands in the courtyards,
on trees, stones, walls,
the dried blood and brains of the dead.
Then go to the ruins, look at the pocked walls,
bad enough before, the sledgehammer made them worse,
smashed stoves, charred stones and bricks
like chronic open-mouthed wounds,
and your legs will sink in feathers,
trip over rubble, piles of torn books and scrolls—
the work of superhuman labor and longing;
don't stand gaping,
go to the road, see the beauty of spring,
breathe in the fragrance of the acacias in blossom,
half-covered in feathers, smelling of blood,
with raging reluctance take in their strange scents,
the joy of spring, don't shirk it;

On April 19–20, 1903 (April 6–7 according to the Julian calendar then in use in the Russian Empire) the Jewish community of Kishinev, the capital of Bessarabia, was attacked in a violent riot in which approximately 50 people were killed, over 500 were wounded, and 1,500 Jewish homes and properties were damaged. This event was to become a metaphor for Jewish suffering at the hands of anti-Semitic savages, as well as a clarion call against intolerance in general for liberal voices in Europe and North America.

Bialik wrote a first "Kishinev" poem ("On the Slaughter") immediately after the event. In the summer of 1903, Bialik was sent to Kishinev by the Jewish Historical Society of Odessa to meet with the local Jewish community in order to document in detail the event and the atrocities. After that five-week visit, Bialik wrote this second Kishinev poem.

[1] Compare with God's instruction to Abram to "get up and go": "And the LORD said to Abram, 'Go forth from your land and your birthplace and your father's house to the land I will show you.'" (Genesis 12:1)

בְּעִיר הַהֲרֵגָה

קוּם לֵךְ לְךָ אֶל עִיר הַהֲרֵגָה וּבָאתָ אֶל־הַחֲצֵרוֹת,
וּבְעֵינֶיךָ תִּרְאֶה וּבְיָדְךָ תְּמַשֵׁשׁ עַל־הַגְּדֵרוֹת
וְעַל הָעֵצִים וְעַל הָאֲבָנִים וְעַל־גַּבֵּי טִיחַ הַכְּתָלִים
אֶת־הַדָּם הַקָּרוּשׁ וְאֶת־הַמֹּחַ הַנִּקְשֶׁה שֶׁל־הַחֲלָלִים.
וּבָאתָ מִשָּׁם אֶל הֶחֳרָבוֹת וּפָסַחְתָּ עַל־הַפְּרָצִים
וְעָבַרְתָּ עַל־הַכְּתָלִים הַנְּקוּבִים וְעַל הַתַּנּוּרִים הַנִּתָּצִים,
בִּמְקוֹם הֶעֱמִיק קָרְקֵר הַמַּפָּץ, הִרְחִיב הִגְדִּיל הַחוֹרִים,
מַחֲשֹׂף הָאֶבֶן הַשְּׁחֹרָה וְעָרוֹת הַלְּבֵנָה הַשְּׂרוּפָה,
וְהֵם נִרְאִים כִּפְיוֹת פְּתוּחִים שֶׁל־פְּצָעִים אֲנוּשִׁים וּשְׁחֹרִים
אֲשֶׁר אֵין לָהֶם תַּקָּנָה עוֹד וְלֹא־תְהִי לָהֶם תְּרוּפָה,
וְטָבְעוּ רַגְלֶיךָ בַּנּוֹצוֹת וְהִתְנַגְּפוּ עַל תִּלֵּי־תִלִּים
שֶׁל־שִׁבְרֵי שְׁבָרִים וּרְסִיסֵי רְסִיסִים וּתְבוּסַת סְפָרִים וּגְוִילִים,
כִּלְיוֹן עֲמַל לֹא־אֱנוֹשׁ וּפְרִי מִשְׁנֶה עֲבוֹדַת פָּרֶךְ;
– וְלֹא־תַּעֲמֹד עַל־הַהֶרֶס וְעָבַרְתָּ מִשָּׁם הַדֶּרֶךְ –
וְלִבְלְבוּ הַשִּׁטִּים לְנֶגְדְּךָ וְזָלְפוּ בְּאַפְּךָ בְּשָׂמִים,
וְצִיצֵיהֶן חֶצְיָם נוֹצוֹת וְרֵיחָן כְּרֵיחַ דָּמִים;

let sunbeams pierce you with sadness, the broken glass
sparkle merrily at your calamity
for the Lord has brought spring and slaughter together—
the sun shone, the acacia bloomed, the killers killed.
Run away to a courtyard,
where one axe decapitated a Jew and his dog,
tossed on the same garbage tip,
their blood rolled in and poked by pigs—
tomorrow's rain will wash it away
and the blood will no longer
scream from the slops
but sink deep into the earth
or quench the thirst of a thorn bush—
and everything will be as nothing,
as if nothing had happened.

* * * *

וְעַל־אַפְּךָ וְעַל־חֲמָתְךָ תָּבִיא קְטָרְתָּן הַזָּרָה
אֶת־עֶדְנַת הָאָבִיב בִּלְבָבְךָ – וְלֹא־תְהִי לְךָ לְזָרָא;
וּבְרִבְבוֹת חִצֵּי זָהָב יְפַלַּח הַשֶּׁמֶשׁ כְּבֵדְךָ
וְשֶׁבַע קַרְנַיִם מִכָּל־רְסִיס זְכוּכִית תִּשְׂמַחְנָה לְאֵידְךָ.
כִּי קָרָא אֲדֹנָי לָאָבִיב וְלַטֶּבַח גַּם־יָחַד:
הַשֶּׁמֶשׁ זָרְחָה, הַשִּׁטָּה פָּרְחָה וְהַשּׁוֹחֵט שָׁחַט.
– וּבָרַחְתָּ וּבָאתָ אֶל־חָצֵר, וְהֶחָצֵר גַּל בּוֹ –
עַל הַגַּל הַזֶּה נֶעֶרְפוּ שְׁנַיִם: יְהוּדִי וְכַלְבּוֹ.
קַרְדֹּם אֶחָד עֲרָפָם וְאֶל־אַשְׁפָּה אַחַת הוּטָלוּ
וּבְעֶרֶב דָּם שְׁנֵיהֶם יְחַטְטוּ חֲזִירִים וְיִתְגּוֹלָלוּ;
מָחָר יֵרֵד גֶּשֶׁם וּסְחָפוֹ אֶל־אַחַד נַחֲלֵי הַבַּתּוֹת –
וְלֹא יִצְעַק עוֹד הַדָּם מִן הַשְּׁפָכִים וְהָאַשְׁפַּתּוֹת,
כִּי בִתְהֹם רַבָּה יֹאבַד אוֹ יַשְׁק נַעֲצוּץ לִרְוָיָה –
וְהַכֹּל יִהְיֶה כְּאַיִן, וְהַכֹּל יָשׁוּב כְּלֹא־הָיָה.

* * * *

To the graveyard, beggars![2]
Dig up the bones of martyred father and brother,
fill your sacks, sling them on backs
and hit the road
to do business at all the fairs;
advertise yourselves at the crossroads so everyone sees,
in the sunshine on filthy rags spread the bones
and sing your hoarse beggar song,
beg the decency of the world!
Beg the pity of *goyim*![3]
Eternal beggars!

And now, what are you doing here,
Son of Man?[4]
Get up, escape to the desert[5]
with sorrow's cup,
rip your soul to bits,
feed your heart to impotent rage,
weep over the boulders,
drown your scream in a storm.

Translated by David Aberbach

[2] Bialik turns his wrath from the destruction to the destroyed, calling them "beggars," "grave diggers," and wandering peasants doing "business at all the fairs."

[3] *Goyim* is a biblical term meaning "nations," which in Yiddish became a popular negative word to describe non-Jews.

[4] *Ben-adam*, "man," is the typical form God uses in addressing Ezekiel: "And He said to me, 'Man, stand on your feet and I shall speak with you.'" (Ezekiel 2:1)

[5] Bialik employs a flurry of biblical terms to chastise Jews for what he regarded as their typical response to crises: fleeing; tearing their garments in mourning; and weeping, which he believed was what Jews had done in the face of disaster.

לְבֵית־הַקְּבָרוֹת, קַבְּצָנִים! וַחֲפַרְתֶּם עַצְמוֹת אֲבוֹתֵיכֶם
וְעַצְמוֹת אֲחֵיכֶם הַקְּדוֹשִׁים וּמִלֵּאתֶם תַּרְמִילֵיכֶם
וַעֲמַסְתֶּם אוֹתָם עַל־שִׁכְמְכֶם וִיצָאתֶם לַדֶּרֶךְ, עֲתִידִים
לַעֲשׂוֹת בָּהֶם סְחוֹרָה בְּכָל־הַיְרִידִים;
וּרְאִיתֶם לָכֶם יָד בְּרֹאשׁ דְּרָכִים, לְעֵין רוֹאִים,
וּשְׁטַחְתֶּם אוֹתָם לַשֶּׁמֶשׁ עַל־סְמַרְטוּטֵיכֶם הַצֹּאִים,
וּבְגָרוֹן נִחָר שִׁירָה קַבְּצָנִית עֲלֵיהֶם תְּשׁוֹרֵרוּ.
וּקְרָאתֶם לְחֶסֶד לְאֻמִּים וְהִתְפַּלַּלְתֶּם לְרַחֲמֵי גוֹיִם,
וְכַאֲשֶׁר פְּשַׁטְתֶּם יָד תִּפְשֹׁטוּ, וְכַאֲשֶׁר שְׁנוֹרַרְתֶּם תְּשְׁנוֹרֵרוּ.

וְעַתָּה מַה־לְּךָ פֹּה, בֶּן־אָדָם, קוּם בְּרַח הַמִּדְבָּרָה
וְנָשֵׂאתָ עִמְּךָ שָׁמָּה אֶת־כּוֹס הַיְּגוֹנִים,
וְקָרַעְתָּ שָׁם אֶת־נַפְשְׁךָ לַעֲשָׂרָה קְרָעִים
וְאֶת־לְבָבְךָ תִּתֵּן מַאֲכָל לַחֲרוֹן אֵין־אוֹנִים,
וְדִמְעָתְךָ הַגְּדוֹלָה הוֹרֵד שָׁם עַל קָדְקֹד הַסְּלָעִים
וְשַׁאֲגָתְךָ הַמָּרָה שַׁלַּח – וְתֹאבַד בִּסְעָרָה.

Shaul Tchernichovsky

(1875–1943)

Shaul Tchernichovsky was born and raised in the village Mykhailivka, located between Crimea and the Ukraine. In distinction from many other writers of his time, Tchernichovsky grew up in the countryside with few other Jews, surrounded by fertile fields and sprawling plains. He received a formal Hebrew education until the age of 10, after which he attended state schools. He pursued medical studies in Heidelberg, Germany, completing his medical degree in Lausanne, Switzerland. Over the years, he lived in St. Petersburg, Kiev, Minsk, Odessa and, for eight months, in the United States, working as a doctor, translator, and poet. Tchernichovsky visited Palestine for the first time in 1925, settled in Tel Aviv in 1931, and ultimately moved to Jerusalem, where he died in 1943. He translated *The Epic of Gilgamesh, The Iliad, The Odyssey*, several plays by Shakespeare and Molière, poetry by Pushkin, and many other classics into Hebrew. His links to the Hebraic classical tradition were mainly to biblical rather than rabbinic texts, and he was equally influenced by the heroic figures of Greek mythology. Tchernichovsky's works reflect a vision of a new Hebrew literature, focused on the majesty of the human spirit and its potential for shaping a new kind of Jew and country.

I Believe

Laugh, laugh, at my dreams,
I the dreamer now speak.
Laugh—while knowing I still believe in humanity,
Because I still believe in you.
Because my soul still thirsts for freedom
I haven't sold out for a golden calf.
Because I will still believe in humanity,
In its spirit, its powerful, empowerment.
That spirit will pulverize binding chains
It will raise us up, with heads held high
No worker will die of hunger
Souls will be nourished with freedom, the poor people with bread.
Laugh, but know I also believe in friendship
I'll believe—I will still find a heart
A heart of my hopes, and of another's hopes,
That will feel joy, and understand anguish.
I will also believe in the future
Even if redemption day seems far away
But when it does come, it will bring peace
And a blessing from nation to nation.
Then, my people will also flourish
And in the land a new generation will arise
One that shakes off its iron shackles.
And eye after eye will see light.

אֲנִי מַאֲמִין

שַׂחֲקִי, שַׂחֲקִי עַל הַחֲלוֹמוֹת,
זוּ אֲנִי הַחוֹלֵם שָׂח.
שַׂחֲקִי כִּי בָאָדָם אַאֲמִין,
כִּי עוֹדֶנִּי מַאֲמִין בָּךְ.
כִּי עוֹד נַפְשִׁי דְּרוֹר שׁוֹאֶפֶת
לֹא מְכַרְתִּיהָ לְעֵגֶל־פָּז,
כִּי עוֹד אַאֲמִין גַּם בָּאָדָם,
גַּם בְּרוּחוֹ, רוּחַ עָז.
רוּחוֹ יַשְׁלִיךְ כַּבְלֵי־הֶבֶל,
יְרוֹמְמֶנּוּ בָּמֳתֵי־עָל;
לֹא בָרָעָב יָמוּת עֹבֵד,
דְּרוֹר – לַנֶּפֶשׁ, פַּת – לַדָּל.
שַׂחֲקִי כִּי גַם בְּרֵעוּת אַאֲמִין,
אַאֲמִין, כִּי עוֹד אֶמְצָא לֵב,
לֵב תִּקְוֹתַי גַּם תִּקְוֹתָיו,
יָחוּשׁ אֹשֶׁר, יָבִין כְּאֵב.
אַאֲמִינָה גַּם בֶּעָתִיד,
אַף אִם יִרְחַק זֶה הַיּוֹם,
אַךְ בּוֹא יָבוֹא – יִשְׂאוּ שָׁלוֹם
אָז וּבְרָכָה לְאֹם מִלְאֹם.
יָשׁוּב יִפְרַח אָז גַּם עַמִּי,
וּבָאָרֶץ יָקוּם דּוֹר,
בַּרְזֶל־כְּבָלָיו יוּסַר מֶנּוּ,
עַיִן־בְּעַיִן יִרְאֶה אוֹר.

It will live, love, work, prosper
A generation living in its land.
Not in the future, not in heaven—
And its spirit shall be eternal.
And then a poet shall sing a new song[1]
With a heart pulsing full of profound beauty
To him, the young one, hovering above my grave,
As flowers blossom into a wreath.

Translated by Gil Troy

[1] "Sing Him a new song, play deftly with joyous shout." (Psalms 33:3)

יִחְיֶה, יֶאֱהַב, יִפְעַל, יַעַשׂ,
דּוֹר בָּאָרֶץ אָמְנָם חָי
לֹא בֶּעָתִיד – בַּשָּׁמַיִם,
חַיֵּי־רוּחַ לוֹ אֵין דָּי.
אָז שִׁיר חָדָשׁ יָשִׁיר מְשׁוֹרֵר,
לְיֹפִי וְנִשְׂגָּב לִבּוֹ עֵר;
לוֹ, לַצָּעִיר, מֵעַל קִבְרִי
פְּרָחִים יִלְקְטוּ לַזֵּר.

Before the Statue of Apollo

To thee I come, O long-abandoned god
Of early moons and unremembered days,
To thee whose reign was in a greener world
Among a race of men divine with youth,
Strong generations of the sons of earth:
To thee, whose right arm broke the bound of heaven
To set on thrones therein thy strongest sons,
Whose proud brows with victorious bays were crowned.
Amongst the gods of old thou wert a god,
Bringing for increase to the mighty earth
A race of demi-gods, instinct with life,
Strange to the children of the house of pain.[1]
A boy-god, passionate and beautiful,
Whose mastery was over the bright sun
And over the dark mysteries of life,
The golden shadow-treasuries of song,
The music of innumerable seas—
A god of joyousness and fresh delight,
Of vigor and the ecstasy of life.

Apollo was the Greek god of the sun, light, medicine, art, prophecy and poetry. Tchernichovsky never saw the original Apollo Statue (which was found in the late 15th-century in Italy and today is housed in the Vatican Apostolic Palace) but a copy of the statue stood in the corridors at the University of Heidelberg, where Tchernichovsky studied between 1899–1903.

[1] Tchernichovsky compares the mighty Greek gods with the passive Israelite God whose children's home is an everlasting place of pain.

לְנֹכַח פֶּסֶל אַפּוֹלוֹ

בָּאתִי עָדֶיךָ, אֵל נִשְׁכָּח מֵעוֹלָם,
אֶל יַרְחֵי־קֶדֶם וְיָמִים אֲחֵרִים,
מוֹלֵךְ עַל זִרְמֵי בְּנֵי־אָדָם רַעֲנַנִּים,
מִשְׁבְּרֵי־אוֹנָם בְּשִׁפְעַת עֲלוּמִים!
אֵל דּוֹר אַדִּירִים וּנְפִילִים בָּאָרֶץ,
כּוֹבֵשׁ בִּזְרוֹעוֹ גַּם גְּבוּל שׁוֹכְנֵי רָמִים
לְמוֹשַׁב גִּבּוֹרִים בְּבָנָיו בַּעֲטֶרֶת
עֲלֵי־הַדַּפְנָה עַל מִצְחָם הַגֵּאֶה,
רוֹדֶה בֶאֱלִילָיו וְנִדְמֶה לָהֵמָּה,
לָשִׁית נוֹסָפוֹת עַל סוֹד מוֹשְׁלֵי חֶבֶל;
דּוֹר אֵל בָּאָרֶץ, שְׂכַר שֶׁפַע הַחַיִּים,
נָכְרִי לְגוֹי חוֹלֶה וּלְבֵית הַכּוֹאֲבִים.
אֵל־נַעַר, נֶאְדָּר, רַעֲנָן, כְּלִיל־יֹפִי,
חוֹלֵשׁ עַל שֶׁמֶשׁ וּמִסְתְּרֵי־חַיִּים
בְּעַרְפִּלֵּי הַשִּׁירָה וּבְגִגְזֵי־גְוָנֶיהָ,
בְּיָם הַנִּגּוּנִים בְּאַלְפֵי גַלֵּימוֹ;
אֵל גִּיל הַחַיִּים בְּכָל עָשְׁרָם וַהֲדָרָם,
תְּקָפָם וְצִפּוּנֵי מַשְׂכִּיּוֹת גַּוְנֵיהֶם.

I am the Jew. Dost thou remember me?
Between us there is enmity forever![2]
Not all the multitudes of ocean's waters,
Storm-linking continent with continent,
Could fill the dark abyss between us yawning.
The heavens and the boundless wilderness
Were short to bridge the wideness set between
My fathers' children and thy worshippers.
And yet behold me! I have wandered far,
By crooked ways, from those that were before me,
And others after me shall know this path.
But amongst those that will return to thee[3]
I was the first to free my soul that groaned
Beneath the agony of generations;
For a day came I would endure no more,
And on that day my spirit burst its chains
And turned again towards the living earth.

The people and its God have aged together!
Passions which strengthlessness had laid to sleep
Start into sudden life again, and break
Their prison of a hundred generations.

[2] The ongoing dialectic between Hellenism and Hebraism.

[3] Return can refer to *teshuvah* or Shivat Zion, see footnote 1, Bialik, from "To the Bird," p. 8.

בָּאתִי עָדֶיךָ, – הַאִם הִכַּרְתָּנִי?
הִנְנִי הַיְּהוּדִי: רִיב לָנוּ לְעוֹלָמִים!...
מִמֵּי־אוֹקְיָנוֹס בֵּין חֶלְקֵי יַבֶּשֶׁת
תְּהוֹם הָרוֹבֶצֶת בֵּינֵינוּ יָבְצֵר
לְמַלֵּא עַד פִּיהָ בִּשְׁאוֹנָם וַהֲמוֹנָם.
שְׁחָקִים וְרַחַב עֲרָבוֹת הֵן קָצְרוּ
מֵהִשְׂתָּרֵעַ בַּפֶּרֶץ, הַמַּפְרִיד
תּוֹרַת אֲבוֹתַי מִדַּת מַעֲרִיצֶיךָ.
עֵינְךָ הָרוֹאָה בִי! יַעַן הִרְחַקְתִּי
לֶכֶת מִכָּל אֲשֶׁר הָיוּ לְפָנַי
וְאַחֲרֵי בִּנְתִיב יֵתַע אָדָם בֶּן־תְּמוּתָה, –
הִנְנִי הָרִאשׁוֹן לַשָּׁבִים אֵלֶיךָ,
רֶגַע בּוֹ קַצְתִּי בִּגְסִיסָה לַדּוֹרוֹת,
בְּמוֹעֵד בּוֹ אֶשְׁבֹּר אַזְקֵי הַנֶּפֶשׁ,
נַפְשִׁי הַחַיָּה, הַדְּבֵקָה בָּאָרֶץ.
זְקַן הָעָם – אֱלֹהָיו זָקְנוּ עִמּוֹ!
רְגָשׁוֹת נִצְמָתִים בִּידֵי חִדְלֵי־אוֹנִים,
קָמוּ לִתְחִיָּה מִמַּסְגֵּר מְאַת דּוֹרוֹת.

The light of God, the light of God is mine!
My blood is clamorous with desire of life.
My limbs, my nerves, my veins, triumphant shout
For life and sunlight.
                    And I come to thee,
And here before thy pedestal I kneel[4]
Because thy symbol is the burning sun.
I kneel to thee, the noble and the true,
Whose strength is in the fullness of the earth,
Whose will is in the fullness of creation,
Whose throne is on the secret founts of being.
I kneel to life, to beauty and to strength,
I kneel to all the passionate desires
Which they, the dead-in-life, the bloodless ones,
The sick, have stifled in the living God,
The God of wonders of the wilderness,
The God of gods, Who took Canaan with storm
Before they bound Him in phylacteries.[5]

Translated by Maurice Samuels

[4] "You shall make you no carved likeness and no image of what is in the heavens above or what is on the earth below or what is in in the waters beneath the earth. You shall not bow to them and you shall not worship them…" (Exodus 20:4–5)

[5] Phylacteries (tefillin) are leather straps worn during the morning prayer service on the head and on the arms to fulfill the commandment, "And you shall bind them as a sign on your hand and they shall be as circlets between your eyes." (Deuteronomy 6:8)

אוֹר־יָהּ לִי! אוֹר־יָהּ! בִּי קוֹרֵא כָּל גֶּרֶם,

חַיִּים, הוֹי חַיִּים! עַל עֶצֶם כָּל עוֹרֵק.

אוֹר־יָהּ וְחַיִּים!

וָאָבֹא אֵלֶיךָ.

בָּאתִי עָדֶיךָ. מוּל פִּסְלְךָ אֶקְדָּה.

פִּסְלְךָ – סֵמֶל הַמָּאוֹר בַּחַיִּים;

אֶקֹּד, אֶכְרָעָה לַטּוֹב וְלַנַּעֲלֶה,

לַאֲשֶׁר הוּא נִשָּׂא בִּמְלֹא כָּל הָעוֹלָם,

לַאֲשֶׁר הוּא נֶהְדָּר בִּמְלֹא כָּל הַבְּרִיאָה,

לַאֲשֶׁר יֵשׁ מְרוֹמָם בְּסוֹד־סוֹדוֹת הַיְצִירָה.

אֶכְרַע לַחַיִּים, לַגְּבוּרָה וְלַיֹּפִי,

אֶכְרַע לְכָל שְׂכִיּוֹת־הַחֶמְדָּה, שֶׁשָּׁדְדוּ

פִּגְרֵי אֲנָשִׁים וּרְקַב זֶרַע אָדָם,

מוֹרְדֵי הַחַיִּים מִיַּד צוּרֵי שַׁדַּי,

אֵל אֱלֹהֵי מִדְבְּרוֹת הַפֶּלִי,

אֵל אֱלֹהֵי כּוֹבְשֵׁי כְּנַעַן בְּסוּפָה, –

וַיַּאַסְרוּהוּ בִּרְצוּעוֹת שֶׁל תְּפִילִין...

They Say There's a Land

They say: There is a land, a land drenched with sun.
Wherefore is that land? Where is that sun?
They say: There is a land, its pillars are seven, seven planets,
　　　blossoming on every hill.[1]
Where is that land, the stars of that hill?
Who shall guide our way, tell me my path?
Already we have passed several deserts and oceans,
Already we have crossed several, our strengths are waning.
How did we err? That we have not been left alone yet?
The same land of sun, that one we have not found.
A land which will fulfill what every individual hoped for,[2]
Everyone who enters, had encountered Akiva.[3]
Peace to you, Akiva! Peace to you, The Rabbi! Where are the saints?
Where is the Maccabee?[4]
Akiva answers; the Rabbi answers:
　　　All of Israel is holy, you are the Maccabee![5]

Translated by Gil Troy

This version of "They Say There is a Land" was the second of two versions of this poem written by Shaul Tchernichovsky in 1923, while living in Berlin. Both versions share the same opening stanza which describes a wonderful new land and then asks how and when that Land will be found. The first version's subsequent stanzas reflect increasing doubt and pessimism in finding that sunny, ideal land.

The second version was written four months later at the request of the leaders of the Herut Movement, who wanted an optimistic uplifting motivational poem for their upcoming International Conference in Berlin in the summer of 1923. In the second version, Tchernichovsky changes the later verses to express the ongoing hope in quest of that land. He read the second version aloud while sitting in the audience of the convention. This second version became a popular song of the pre-state Jewish *Yishuv* in Palestine.

[1] "Wisdom has built her house, she has hewn her pillars, seven." (Proverbs 9:1) "Seven" does not necessarily refer to the number of arches, but rather to the symbolic significance of the number seven in Jewish and Greek mythology.

אוֹמְרִים: יֶשְׁנָה אֶרֶץ...

"שָׁלוֹם לְךָ, עֲקִיבָא!	אוֹמְרִים יֶשְׁנָה אֶרֶץ
שָׁלוֹם לְךָ, רַבִּי!	אֶרֶץ רְוַת שֶׁמֶשׁ...
אֵיפֹה הֵם הַקְּדוֹשִׁים,	אַיֵּה אוֹתָהּ אֶרֶץ?
אֵיפֹה הַמַּכַּבִּי?"	אֵיפֹה אוֹתוֹ שֶׁמֶשׁ?
עוֹנֶה לוֹ עֲקִיבָא,	אוֹמְרִים: יֶשְׁנָה אֶרֶץ
אוֹמֵר לוֹ הָרַבִּי:	עַמּוּדֶיהָ שִׁבְעָה,
"כָּל יִשְׂרָאֵל קְדוֹשִׁים,	שִׁבְעָה כּוֹכְבֵי־לֶכֶת
אַתָּה הַמַּכַּבִּי!"	צָצִים עַל כָּל גִּבְעָה.
	אֶרֶץ – בָּהּ יְקֻיַּם
	כָּל אֲשֶׁר אִישׁ קִוָּה,
	נִכְנַס כָּל הַנִּכְנָס –
	פָּגַע בּוֹ עֲקִיבָא.

[2] Reference to the anthem, "Hatikvah" (see above).

[3] Rabbi Akiva was a central figure in the Talmud who was martyred in 135 CE at the hands of the Romans during the Bar Kochva rebellion against Rome. While Rabbi Akiva is generally depicted as one of the unique intellectual, spiritual, and moral teachers in Jewish history, Tchernichovsky focuses on Akiva as a heroic nationalist. See Barry W. Holtz, *Rabbi Akiva Sage of the Talmud* (New Haven: Yale University Press, 2017).

[4] The Maccabees refer to the family (led by Judah) that spearheaded the military battle against the Greeks in 167 BCE and established the Hasmonean dynasty (which lasted until 37 BCE). Both the Maccabean victory and Akiva's martyrdom are regarded as significant historical exemplars of the Israelite struggle for sovereignty in the Land of Israel.

[5] This version of the poem concludes with an upbeat charge to the people (participants in the Herut Conference) to rise to the occasion and to see themselves as heirs to the heroism of the Maccabees.

Rahel Bluwstein

(1890–1931)

Rahel Bluwstein was born in Saratov in Imperial Russia and died in Tel Aviv at the age of 41 from tuberculosis. She grew up in an affluent family and attended a Russian-speaking Hebrew primary school and a secular secondary school, where her interest in art and poetry was awakened. At the age of 19, Rahel and her sister traveled to Palestine, where she devoted herself to learning Hebrew and studying the Bible, later moving to the Kibbutz Kinneret on the shore of the Sea of Galilee, where she joined an all-women's working group. In 1913, she moved to France to study agronomy and then, during the First World War, to Odessa, where she worked with refugee children and translated the writings of Bialik and others into Russian. It was there that she contracted tuberculosis, which was to plague her for the rest of her life. In 1918, Rahel returned to Palestine and, after a brief stay at Kibbutz Degania near the Sea of Galilee, she was asked to leave since the communal leadership determined that she represented a health risk to the others. Rahel moved to a modest apartment near the sea in Tel Aviv, where she devoted herself to writing poetry until her death. Her writings combine a unique, brief lyrical style with moving pastoral scenes, and her colloquial Hebrew distinguished her from Bialik's and Tchernichovsky's grandiose poetry, often studded with biblical and classical references. Rahel is buried in the cemetery of Kibbutz Kinneret on the western shore of the Sea of Galilee, where many visitors pay tribute to her life and read from a volume of her poems kept in a box beside her grave.

"Was it only a dream..."

Was it only a dream? Was it I?
Was it I who long ago
rose with the dawn to fill the fields
by the sweat of my brow?[1]

Was it I who on long, sultry days
of harvesting
on a high wagon loaded with sheaves
would sing?

Was it I who bathed in the innocent blue[2]
—under a peaceful sky—
Of my Galilee, my own Galilee?
Was it only a dream? Was it I?

Translated by Robert Friend

[1] "By the sweat of your brow shall you eat bread till you return to the soil, for from there were you taken, for dust you are and to dust shall you return." (Genesis 3:19) The phrase 'sweat of your brow' is from the story of Adam and Eve's banishment from the Garden of Eden, which may well echo the feeling of the poet being forced to leave her beloved Sea of Galilee.

[2] The word *taharti* (literally, "I purified myself") might be a comparison of bathing in the *Kineret* to the ritual of submerging oneself in the *mikveh* (ritual bath).

וְאוּלַי לֹא הָיוּ הַדְּבָרִים...

וְאוּלַי לֹא הָיוּ הַדְּבָרִים מֵעוֹלָם,
אוּלַי
מֵעוֹלָם לֹא הִשְׁכַּמְתִּי עִם שַׁחַר לַגָּן,
לְעָבְדוֹ בְּזֵעַת־אַפִּי?

מֵעוֹלָם, בְּיָמִים אֲרֻכִּים וְיוֹקְדִים
שֶׁל קָצִיר,
בְּמֵרוֹמֵי עֲגָלָה עֲמוּסַת אֲלֻמּוֹת
לֹא נָתַתִּי קוֹלִי בְּשִׁיר?

מֵעוֹלָם לֹא טָהַרְתִּי בִּתְכֵלֶת שׁוֹקֵטָה
וּבְתֹם
שֶׁל כִּנֶּרֶת שֶׁלִּי... הוֹי, כִּנֶּרֶת שֶׁלִּי,
הֶהָיִית, אוֹ חָלַמְתִּי חֲלוֹם?

"Here on earth…"

Here on the earth — not in high clouds —
On this mother earth that is close:
To sorrow in her sadness, exult in her meager joy
That knows, so well, how to console.

Not nebulous tomorrow but today: solid, warm, mighty,
Today materialized in the hand:
Of this single, short day to drink deep
Here in our own land.

Before night falls — come, oh come all!
A unified stubborn effort, awake
With a thousand arms. Is it impossible to roll
The stone from the mouth of the well?[1]

Translated by Ruth Finer Mintz

[1] The Book of Genesis tells the story of Rachel, wife of Jacob, who "…came with her father's sheep, for she was a shepherdess. And it happened when Jacob saw Rachel…he stepped forward and rolled the stone from the mouth of the well and watered the sheep of Laban his mother's brother." (Genesis 29:9–10) Rahel suggests that the arms of the modern pioneers in Palestine can perform similar acts of valor.

כָּאן עַל פְּנֵי הָאֲדָמָה

כָּאן עַל פְּנֵי אֲדָמָה – לֹא בֶּעָבִים, מֵעָל –
עַל פְּנֵי אֲדָמָה הַקְּרוֹבָה, הָאֵם;
לְהֵעָצֵב בְּעָצְבָּה וְלָגִיל בְּגִילָה הַדַּל
הַיּוֹדֵעַ כָּל כָּךְ לְנַחֵם.

לֹא עַרְפִלֵּי מָחָר – הַיּוֹם הַמּוּמָשׁ בַּיָּד,
הַיּוֹם הַמּוּצָק, הֶחָם, הָאֵיתָן;
לִרְווֹת אֶת הַיּוֹם הַזֶּה, הַקָּצָר, הָאֶחָד,
עַל פְּנֵי אַדְמָתֵנוּ כָּאן.

בְּטֶרֶם אָתָא הַלֵּיל – בּוֹאוּ, בּוֹאוּ הַכֹּל!
מַאֲמָץ מְאֻחָד, עַקְשָׁנִי וָעֵר
שֶׁל אֶלֶף זְרוֹעוֹת. הַאֻמְנָם יִבָּצֵר לָגֹל
אֶת הָאֶבֶן מִפִּי הַבְּאֵר?

"Love was late in coming..."

Love was late in coming, and coming[1]
didn't dare call out: I am here,[2]
while she knocked on the doors of the heart,
and stood as a poor man stands,
hands silently stretched out.
Her look was sad and imploring,
submissive and filled with doubt.

Pale are the candles, therefore,
that I have lit for her,
pale as the last of flowers
in the autumn light;
hesitant my joy, therefore,
quiet and in pain
like the pain of hope disappointed
or waiting, waiting in vain.

Translated by Robert Friend

[1] The word *ahavah*, "love," does not appear in the Hebrew poem. Instead, the female-speaker in the poem uses the phrase "she was late in coming." In the Hebrew poem, the word "she" could be referring to the word "love," but it is not explicitly mentioned.

[2] In the Pentateuch, *hineini*, "here I am," is the traditional response when God calls upon a person by name. For example: "And it happened after these things that God tested Abraham. And He said to him, 'Abraham!' and he said, 'Here I am.'" (Genesis 22:1) and "And the LORD saw that he had turned aside to see, and God called to him from the midst of the bush and said, 'Moses, Moses!' And he said, 'Here I am.'" (Exodus 3:4)

הִיא אֶחֲרָה לָבוֹא

הִיא אֶחֲרָה לָבוֹא וּבְבוֹאָהּ לֹא הֵעֵזָה,
לֹא הֵעֵזָה לִקְרֹא: הִנְנִי! בְּדָפְקָהּ עַל דַּלְתוֹת הַלֵּב ;
כַּעֲמֹד עֲנִיָּה עָמְדָה, וְיָדֶיהָ דּוּמָם הוֹשִׁיטָה;
וְעֶצֶב הָיָה מַבָּטָהּ, מִתְחַנֵּן, נִכְנָע וְעָצֵב.

וְעַל כֵּן חֹרִים הַנֵּרוֹת אֲשֶׁר לִכְבוֹדָהּ הֶעֱלֵיתִי,
כְּאַחֲרוֹנֵי נְגֹהוֹת בְּהַאֲפִיר דְּמְדּוּמֵי סְתָו;
וְעַל כֵּן חֲרִישִׁית שִׂמְחָתִי, חֲרִישִׁית, מְהֻסֶּסֶת, מַדְאֶבֶת,
כְּהַדְאֵב תִּקְוָה נִכְזָבָה, כֵּעֲנוּת צִפִּיַּת־שָׁוְא.

ISRAEL:
VOICES
FROM
WITHIN

Section 2

From Vision to Statehood

The foundations of a Jewish state in Palestine were created in the years between the beginning of the British Mandate, as outlined in the San Remo conference of 1920, and the Declaration of Independence of the State of Israel on May 14, 1948. This period was marked by an era of increased Jewish immigration, ongoing rural and urban growth, and an emerging infrastructure that would become the State of Israel. These dynamics took place amid unrelenting conflict with the local Arab population and the tragedy of the Holocaust in the third and fourth decades of the twentieth century.

The poets and writers of this era were generally immigrants from Central and Eastern Europe and Russia. The majority had received both a classical Jewish and Western education. Their Hebrew and Judaic literacy was usually shaped by family life, prayer, study of religious Jewish texts, and an engagement with the newly budding secular Hebrew literature. Their general cultural and intellectual education was acquired in secondary school, academia, and individual study and immersion. While many of these poets abandoned traditional Jewish theology and religious practice, their writings still incorporated language, concepts, and references derived from traditional Jewish literature and life. The Hebrew wielded by of most of this group was essentially *written* rather than *spoken* (what the Swiss linguist Ferdinand de Saussure[1] denoted as *"langue"* as opposed to *"parole"*) and they wrote in a "grand Hebrew" style, aimed at inspiring, igniting, and sometimes enraging their readers.

The poems penned by these writers are in turn "heavy with silence," (Goldberg) and yet they burn with the fervent glow of prophecy and the crash of the blacksmith's hammer (Grinberg). They serenade the land's "golden tapered sky," (Shlonsky) but also declare themselves "orphaned tonight" as they lie down in a leaky, windy, and unlit pioneer tent in the Galilee (Shlonsky). While some of these poets celebrated the dawning pioneer spirit of the Upper Galilee, they themselves were most likely to be found in the cafés and cultural centers of *Bauhaus* Tel Aviv. Jerusalem was to retain its persona as the "Holy City".

Some of these poets were to become voices listened to by the political leadership of the *Yishuv* and others became popular folk figures whose poems became well-known anthems and songs. The poetry of this generation presents an emotional kaleidoscope of images depicting the joys, sorrows, realities and—perhaps, above all—the dreams and the aspirations of a collective engaged in a grand and historic endeavor.

---

[1] De Saussure used the term *"langue"* to refer to systematic rules and principles of written language while *"parole"* referred to the spoken and written language used in everyday life and in the street. *"Langue"* is about system and structure and *"parole"* is about the use of language in everyday talking and living. See Ferdinand De Saussure, *Course in General Linguistics* (London: Hard Press Publishing, 2013).

BACKGROUND:

Shapira, *Israel: A History*, 67–135.

Gordis, *Israel: A Concise History of a Nation Reborn*, 89–162.

Troy, *The Zionist Ideas*. 3–35.

Avraham Shlonsky

(1900–1973)

Avraham Shlonsky, born in Poltava, Ukraine, was one of the major figures shaping modern Hebrew poetry. His father had a Chabad Hasidic upbringing and his mother was a Russian revolutionary. Shlonsky received both a religious and a secular Hebrew education in his youth. At the age of 13, he was sent to Palestine to study at the Herzliya Hebrew Gymnasium, returning to Ukraine at the outbreak of the First World War. He settled permanently in Palestine in 1921. His influence was felt in a variety of spheres—as a poet, editor, translator and author of children's books. His poetry is characterized by contemporary themes, reflecting an innovative transformation that injected modern meaning into traditional verses. "He spoke to us," Lea Goldberg wrote, "in our language and in the language of our times." He was part of a group of poets (which included Goldberg and Alterman) who challenged the hegemony of Bialik in 20th century Hebrew poetry. Shlonsky was a recipient of all of Israel's major prizes for poetry.

Toil

Dress me, good (pious) mother, in a glorious coat of many colors[1]
And with dawn lead me to toil.[2]

My country wraps itself in light as in a prayer shawl.[3]
Houses stand out like phylacteries.
And like phylactery straps, the highways that palms have paved
    glide down.[4]

Here the beautiful town[5] prays matins to its creator
And among the creators
Is your son, Abraham,
A hymn-writer—road-paver in Israel.

[1] "And Israel loved Joseph more than all his sons, for he was the child of his old age, and he made him an ornamented tunic [coat of many colors]." (Genesis 37:3)

[2] In the Bible, *amal* refers to toil that encompasses travail and suffering, "What gain is there for man in all his toil that he toils under the sun." (Ecclesiastes 1:3)

[3] The "prayer shawl" is the *tallit*, a shawl-like garment worn during prayer. *Tefillin* are phylacteries—small boxes attached by leather straps to the arm and to the head and worn in prayer as described in the *Shema* prayer: "And these words that I charge you today shall be upon your heart … And you shall bind them as a sign on your hand and they shall be as circlets between your eyes." (Deuteronomy 6:6–8)

[4] The religious ritual of wearing *tefillin* is transformed into the secular ritual of building a Jewish homeland, with the square head part of *tefillin* boxes symbolizing houses being built on hills and the black leather arm straps of the *tefillin* representing new roads in the country.

[5] The word *kirya* was generally used in the Bible to refer to Jerusalem. Here—and in contemporary Hebrew—it refers to a new settlement, neighborhood or town.

עָמָל

הַלְבִּישִׁינִי, אִמָּא כְּשֵׁרָה, כְּתֹנֶת־פַּסִּים לְתִפְאֶרֶת
וְעִם שַׁחֲרִית הוֹבִילִינִי אֱלֵי עָמָל.

עוֹטְפָה אַרְצִי אוֹר כַּטַּלִּית.
בָּתִּים נִצְּבוּ כַּטּוֹטָפוֹת.
וְכִרְצוּעַת־תְּפִלִּין גּוֹלְשִׁים כְּבִישִׁים, סָלְלוּ כַּפַּיִם.

תְּפִלַּת שַׁחֲרִית כֹּה תִתְפַּלֵּל קִרְיָה נָאָה אֱלֵי בּוֹרְאָהּ.
וּבַבּוֹרְאִים
בְּנֵךְ אַבְרָהָם,
פַּיְטָן סוֹלֵל בְּיִשְׂרָאֵל.

And in the evening, at sunset, father shall return from his labors
And like a prayer,[6] he will whisper with contentment:
My darling son Abraham,
Skin and veins and bones.
Hallelujah![7]

Dress me, good (pious) mother, in a glorious coat of many colors
And with dawn lead me
To toil.[8]

Translated by Shimon Sandbank and John Felsteiner

[6] In earlier times, a father would participate in the evening prayer service at dusk. Now the word *avoda*—which traditionally referred to part of the evening prayer ritual—is transformed into the secular return from physical labor.

[7] *Hallelujah* is a word used in the Book of Psalms. Its literal meaning is "praise God" (some have suggested that it might also be a kind of musical punctuation sign, since the psalms were generally sung).

[8] Shlonsky concludes the poem with the new notion of "toil" as physical rebuilding and creation rather than verbal piety in words and prayer.

וּבָעֶרֶב בֵּין הַשְּׁמָשׁוֹת יָשׁוּב אַבָּא מִסִּבְלוֹתָיו
וְכִתְפִלָּה יִלְחַשׁ נַחַת:
הַבֵּן יַקִּיר לִי אַבְרָהָם,
עוֹר וְגִידִים וַעֲצָמוֹת.
הַלְלוּיָהּ.

הַלְבִּישִׁינִי, אִמָּא כְּשֵׁרָה, כְּתֹנֶת־פַּסִּים לְתִפְאֶרֶת
וְעִם שַׁחֲרִית הוֹבִילִינִי
אֱלֵי עָמָל.

Mr. X Speaks about His Neighborhood

The building I live in has 5 floors[1]
And all its windows are yawned to what's opposite,
Like the faces of those who stand before the mirror.

There are 70 bus lines in my city,
All of them up to [the point of] choking and up to [the point of] the
   stinking of bodies.
They travel
They travel
They travel to the heart of the city
As if it were impossible to die from boredom here also—
In my own neighborhood.

The word *ploni* is used in the title to refer to an anonymous person or place (Ruth 4:1; I
Samuel 21:3). Alternative English versions of this poem translate *ploni* as either "John Doe" or
"Mr. X."

[1] Shlonsky uses actual numbers on this poem, perhaps to emphasize the impersonal
nature of demarcating houses in the modern metropolis.

נְאֻם פְּלוֹנִי עַל שְׁכוּנָתוֹ

בֵּית־מְגוּרַי הוּא בֶּן 5 קוֹמוֹת, –
וְכָל חַלּוֹנוֹתָיו מְפֻהָקִים אֶל שֶׁכְּנֶגֶד,
כִּפְנֵי הַנִּצָּבִים אֶל מוּל רְאִי.

70 קַוֵּי אוֹטוֹבּוּסִים בְּעִירִי,
וְכֻלָּם עַד מַחְנָק וְעַד סְרָחוֹן הַגּוּפִים.
הֵם נוֹסְעִים
הֵם נוֹסְעִים
הֵם נוֹסְעִים אֶל לֵב הַכְּרַךְ,
כְּאִלּוּ אִי־אֶפְשָׁר לִגְווֹעַ מִשִּׁעֲמוּם גַּם כָּאן, –
בִּשְׁכוּנָתִי שֶׁלִּי.

My neighborhood is very small,
Yet it contains all the births and deaths,
And whatever [there is] between birth and death
That is in the world's cities—
Even children, who spin "flying saucer" discs marvelously,
And 3 movie theatres.
If I did not find the boredom that I have in my own home quite enough,
I would go to one of them.

The building I live in has 5 floors—
That woman who leaped from the window opposite
Found 3 to be quite enough.[2]

Translated by Shimon Sandbank and John Felsteiner

[2] In contrast to the rhetoric of Tel Aviv as a thriving, new, all-Hebrew city, Shlonsky depicts it as the typical maze of any modern metropolis, which like all other big cities is sometimes a venue for inexplicable, (and in contrast to the Masada myth of martyrdom) lonely suicides.

שְׁכוּנָתִי שֶׁלִּי הִיא קְטַנָּה מְאֹד,

אַךְ יֵשׁ בָּהּ כָּל הַלֵּדוֹת וְהַמִּיתוֹת,

וְכָל שֶׁבֵּין לֵדָה לְמָוֶת

שֶׁיֵּשׁ בְּכַרְכֵּי הָעוֹלָם, –

אֲפִילוּ תִּינוֹקוֹת, הַמְּסוֹבְבִים לְהַפְלִיא צַלַּחַת–מְעוֹפֶפֶת,

וּ‑3 בָּתֵּי‑קוֹלְנוֹעַ.

לוּלֵא הִסְתַּפַּקְתִּי בַּשִּׁעֲמוּם שֶׁיֵּשׁ לִי בְּבֵיתִי,

הָיִיתִי הוֹלֵךְ לְאֶחָד מֵהֶם.

בֵּית‑מְגוּרִי הוּא בֶּן 5 קוֹמוֹת, –

זוֹ שֶׁקָּפְצָה מִן הַחַלּוֹן שֶׁכְּנֶגֶד

נִסְתַּפְּקָה בְּ‑3 בִּלְבַד. –

Uri Zvi Grinberg

(1896–1981)

Uri Zvi Grinberg was born in Galicia in Eastern Europe, served in the Austro-Hungarian army in the First World War, and settled in Palestine in 1924. Grinberg became one of the leading intellectual figures in the Revisionist Zionist movement, and not only was he one of the pre-state's most widely read and honored poets, but he also exerted an important influence on emergent literary and political discussion and debate. His poetry is marked by passion, fire, and a prophetic-like fervor. He has been regarded as an important spokesperson of a quasi-mystical belief in Zionism as the fulfillment of a historical Jewish identity. His poetic energy is often regarded as fueled by his intense ideological Zionist viewpoint. In 1949, he was elected a member of the Israeli Knesset (Parliament). He was a seminal figure in pre-state Palestine.

*

Like chapters of prophecy[1] my days burn, in all the revelations,
And my body between them's a block of metal for smelting,[2]
And over me stands my God, the Smith, who hits hard:
Each wound that Time has opened in me opens its mouth[3] to him
And pours forth in a shower of sparks the intrinsic fire.

This is my just lot—until dusk on the road.
And when I return to throw my beaten block on a bed,
My mouth is an open wound,
And naked I speak with my God:
You worked hard.[4]
Now it is night; come, let us both rest.

Translated by Robert Mezey and Ben Zion Gold

[1] Grinberg uses the fiery words of the prophets to describe the creation of the new homeland.

[2] "Therefore, thus said the Master, the LORD: Inasmuch as they all have become dross, therefore will I gather them into Jerusalem, a gathering of silver and bronze and iron and lead and tin into the kiln to fan fire upon it for smelting. So will I gather My anger and My wrath and fan the fire and smelt you." (Ezekiel 22:19–20)

[3] "Is not My word like fire, said the LORD, and like a hammer splitting rock?" (Jeremiah 23:29–30)

[4] Perhaps an ironic allusion to Elijah (I Kings 19:4) and Jonah (Jonah 4:3–4) who asked to die when they could no longer bear the challenges of their role and God's.

*

כִּפְרָקַי נְבוּאָה בּוֹעֲרִים יְמוֹתַי בְּכָל הַגֹּלְוֹּיִם
וְגוּפִי בֵּינֵיהֶם כְּגוּשׁ הַמַּתֶּכֶת לְהַתּוּךְ.
וְעָלַי עוֹמֵד אֵלִי הַנַּפָּח וּמַכֶּה בִגְבוּרָה:
כָּל פֶּצַע, שֶׁחָתַךְ הַזְּמַן בִּי, פּוֹתֵחַ לוֹ חִתּוּךְ
וּפוֹלֵט בִּגְצֵי רְגָעִים הָאֵשׁ הָעֲצוּרָה.

זֶהוּ גּוֹרָלִי־מִשְׁפָּטִי עַד עֶרֶב בַּדֶּרֶךְ.
וּבְשׁוּבִי לְהַטִּיל אֶת גּוּשִׁי הַמֻּכֶּה עַל עֶרֶשׂ,
פִּי – פֶּצַע פָּתוּחַ.
וְעֵירֹם אֲדַבֵּר עִם אֵלִי: עָבַדְתָּ בְּפָרֶךְ.
עַתָּה בָּא לַיְלָה; תֵּן – שְׁנֵינוּ נָנוּחַ.

מתוך המחזור: "עִם אֵלִי הַנַּפָּח" (כל כתביו / אורי צבי גרינברג. ירושלים, מוסד ביאליק, תשנ"א-תשע"ו 1991–2016).

*

Like a woman who knows that her body entices me,
God taunts me, Flee if you can! But I can't flee,
For when I turn away from him, angry and heartsick,
With a vow on my lips like a burning coal:
I will not see him again—[1]

I can't do it,
                              I turn back
And knock on his door,[2]
Tortured with longing

As though he had sent me a love letter.

Translated by Robert Mezey and Ben Zion Gold

[1] The poem reflects the irony of many modern Zionist poets who nonetheless express their ideas in traditional Hebraic language.

[2] These words refer to one of the great statements of romantic love in the biblical volume, the Song of Songs: "I was asleep but my heart was awake: Hark! my lover knocks. — Open for me, my sister, my friend, my dove, my perfect one. For my head is drenched with dew, my locks with the drops of the night." (Song of Songs 5:2)

*

כְּמוֹ אִשָּׁה הַיּוֹדְעָה כִּי רַבּוּ עָלַי קְסָמֶיהָ,
יִלְעַג לִי אֵלִי: בְּרַח אִם רַק תּוּכַל!
וְלִבְרֹחַ לֹא אוּכַל.

כִּי בְּבָרְחִי מִמֶּנּוּ בְּחֵמָה נוֹאֶשֶׁת
וּבְנֶדֶר בְּפִי, כְּנַחֶלֶת לוֹחֶשֶׁת:
"לֹא אוֹסִיף רְאוֹתוֹ!"

אֲנִי שָׁב אֵלָיו שֵׁנִית
וְדוֹפֵק עַל דְּלָתָיו,
כְּאוֹהֵב הַמְיַסֵּר.

כְּאִלּוּ אִגֶּרֶת אֲהָבִים לִי כָּתַב.

מתוך המחזור "עִם אֵלִי הַנַּפָּח" (כל כתביו / אורי צבי גרינברג. ירושלים, מוסד ביאליק, תשנ"א-תשע"ו 1991–2016).

*

We were not likened to dogs among the Gentiles — They pity a dog.
Caress, even kiss him with the Gentile mouth. For like a puppy
Fondled at home, they pamper it, delight in it always:
And when this dog dies — how very much the Gentiles mourn him!

We were not led like sheep to the slaughter[1] in the boxcars
For like leprous sheep they led us to extinction
Over all the beautiful landscapes of Europe...
The Gentiles did not handle their sheep as they handled our bodies:
Before slaughter they did not pull out the teeth of their sheep:
They did not strip the wool from their bodies as they did to us:
They did not push the sheep into the fire to make ash of the living
And to scatter the ashes over streams and sewers.

Are there other analogies to this, our disaster that came to us at their hands?
There are no other analogies (all words are shades of shadow)—
Therein lies the horrifying phrase: No other analogies!
For every cruel torture that man may yet do to man in a Gentile country—
He who comes to compare will state: He was tortured like a Jew.
Every fright, every terror, every loneliness, every chagrin,
Every murmuring, weeping in the world
He who compares will say: This analogy is of the Jewish kind.

There is no recompense for our disaster, for its circumference is the world:
The whole culture of the Gentile Kingdoms to its peak—through our blood:
And all its conscience—through our weeping.

Translated by Ruth Finer Mintz

[1] The phrase "like sheep to the slaughter" is both a tragic expression of the plight of the Jews and their suffering as well as a pejorative term critiquing Jewish passivity.

*

לֹא נִדְמֵינוּ לַכְּלָבִים בַּגּוֹיִים... כִּי הֵן כֶּלֶב אֶצְלָם יְרֻחַם
יְלֻטַּף וְיֵשׁ גַּם שֶׁיִּנָּשֵׁק מִפִּי גּוֹי, כִּי כַוָּלָד
חָמוּד בְּבֵיתוֹ יְפַנְּקֵהוּ וְשָׂשׂ בּוֹ תָּמִיד;
וּבְמוֹת כֶּלֶב זֶה, מַה מְּאֹד יֶאֱבַל עָלָיו גּוֹי!

לֹא הוּבַלְנוּ כַצֹּאן לְטִבְחָה בְּקְרוֹנוֹת רַכָּבוֹת
כִּי כַצֹּאן מְצֹרָע הוֹבִילוּנוּ לְמוֹ כִלְיָה
דֶּרֶךְ כָּל הַנּוֹפִים הַיָּפִים בְּאֵירֹפָּה....
לֹא כִלְצֹאנָם עָשׂוּ הַגּוֹיִים בְּגוּפֵנוּ:
בְּטֶרֶם שְׁחִיטָה לֹא עָקְרוּ אֶת שִׁנֵּי הַצֹּאן:
לֹא פָּשְׁטוּ מִגּוּפָם אֶת צַמְרָם כַּאֲשֶׁר לָנוּ עָשׂוּ:
לֹא דָחֲפוּ אֶת הַצֹּאן אֶל הָאֵשׁ לַעֲשׂוֹת אֵפֶר מִן חַי
וְלִזְרוֹת אֶת הָאֵפֶר אֶל פְּנֵי נְחָלִים וּבִיבִים...

הֲיֵשׁ מְשָׁלִים עוֹד לְזֶה אֲסוֹנֵנוּ שֶׁבָּא לָן מִיָּדָם?
אֵין עוֹד מְשָׁלִים. (כָּל הַמִּלִּים צֵאֱלֵי צְלָלִים) –
וּבְזֶה הַבִּטּוּי הַמַּחֲרִיד: אֵין עוֹד מְשָׁלִים!
כָּל עִנּוּי אַכְזָר שֶׁיֵּעָשֶׂה בֶן אָדָם בְּאֶרֶץ גּוֹיִית לְאָדָם,
יְדַמֵּהוּ הַבָּא־לְהַמְשִׁיל: הוּא עָנָה כִיהוּדִי.
כָּל מָגוֹר כָּל זְוָעָה כָּל בְּדִידוּת כָּל עָגְמָה
כָּל בְּכִיָה הוֹמִיָה בָּעוֹלָם
יֹאמַר הַמַּמְשִׁיל: זֶה מָשָׁל מִן הַמִּין הַיְהוּדִי.

אֵין שָׁלֵם לַאֲסוֹנֵנוּ כִּי מִדַּת הֶקֵּפוֹ הוּא עוֹלָם:
כָּל תַּרְבּוּת מַלְכֻיוֹת הַגּוֹיִים עַד שִׂיאָהּ – בְּדָמֵנוּ
וְכָל מַצְפּוּנָהּ – בְּבִכְיֵנוּ.

מתוך המחזור "לֵאלֹהִים בְּאֵירֹפָּה"

Nathan Alterman

(1910–1970)

Born in Warsaw, Alterman moved with his family to Tel Aviv at the age of 15. He became a prominent and influential Israeli poet, playwright, journalist and public voice in the years leading up to statehood and thereafter. His poetry included neo-romantic, patriotic-melodramatic, and satirical verse. Some of his poems were put to music and became part of the "songbook" of the new state. Alterman translated Shakespeare, Molière, Racine, and others into Hebrew and Yiddish. His weekly column in verse (*HaTur Hashvi'i*) in the weekend edition of the pre-state Labor-movement newspaper *Davar* was to have a significant influence on political leaders, intellectuals, and the larger public of the emergent state, and he was regarded as an artistic voice that shaped the national cause.

The Silver Platter

> "The state will not be given to the Jewish people
> on a silver platter."
> — Chaim Weizmann

And the land quiets, the crimson sky slowly dimming over
    smoking frontiers[1]
And the nation arises, heartbroken but breathing,
To receive the miracle, the only one, there is no other....

As the ceremony approaches, it will rise amid the moon, standing erect
    in terror and joy. When across from it a young man and woman
    emerge and slowly, slowly march toward the people.

Dressed in battle gear, dirty,
Shoes heavy with grime, they climb the path quietly.
They didn't change their clothes, they didn't wipe their brows,[2]
Still bone weary from days and nights in the battlefield

The story of this poem begins on December 15, 1947 in Atlantic City, New Jersey, where Zionist leader Chaim Weizmann was speaking to a gathering of the United Jewish Appeal (UJA) to raise funds for the defense of the Yishuv. In his speech, Weizmann said, "The state will not be given to the Jewish people on a silver platter." The poet Nathan Alterman took these words and wrote the poem, *"Magash HaKesef"* ("The Silver Platter"), which he published on December 19, 1947 in his weekly column in the *Davar* newspaper.

[1] "And Midian was laid low before Israel, and they no longer lifted their heads, and the land was quiet forty years." (Judges 8:28)

[2] "By the sweat of your brow shall you eat bread till you return to the soil, for from there you were taken, for dust you are and to dust shall you return." (Genesis 3:19)

מַגַּש הַכֶּסֶף

"אֵין מְדִינָה נִתֶּנֶת לְעַם
עַל מַגָּשׁ שֶׁל כֶּסֶף" –
חיים וייצמן

...וְהָאָרֶץ תִּשְׁקֹט. עֵין שָׁמַיִם אוֹדֶמֶת
תְּעַמְעֵם לְאַטָּה
עַל גְּבוּלוֹת עֲשֵׁנִים.
וְאֻמָּה הַעֲמֹד – קְרוּעַת לֵב אַךְ נוֹשֶׁמֶת ... –
לְקַבֵּל אֶת הַנֵּס
הָאֶחָד אֵין שֵׁנִי...

הִיא לַטֶּקֶס תִּכּוֹן. הִיא תָקוּם לְמוּל סַהַר
וְעָמְדָה, טֶרֶם־יוֹם, עוֹטָה חַג וְאֵימָה.
– – אָז מִנֶּגֶד יֵצְאוּ
נַעֲרָה וָנַעַר
וְאַט־אַט יִצְעֲדוּ הֵם אֶל מוּל הָאֻמָּה.

לוֹבְשֵׁי חֹל וַחֲגוֹר, וְכִבְדֵי נַעֲלַיִם,
בַּנָּתִיב יַעֲלוּ הֵם
הָלוֹךְ וְהַחֲרֵשׁ.
לֹא הֶחְלִיפוּ בִגְדָם, לֹא מָחוּ עוֹד בַּמַּיִם
אֶת עִקְבוֹת יוֹם־הַפֶּרֶךְ וְלֵיל קַו־הָאֵשׁ.

Interminably exhausted, abstainers from rest,
Yet wearing their youth like dew glistening on their head.
Silently, the two approach and stand immobile at attention, giving no
     sign of living or dying.

Then, enveloped in tears and wonder, the nation will ask:
     "Who are you?"
And the two will reply quietly: "We are the silver platter on which the
     Jewish state was given."

This they will say and fall back encased in shadows
And the rest will be told in Israel's chronicles.

Translated by Gil Troy

עֲיֵפִים עַד בְּלִי קֵץ, נְזִירִים מִמַּרְגּוֹעַ,
וְנוֹטְפִים טַלְלֵי נְעוּרִים עִבְרִיִּים – –
דֹּם הַשָּׁנַיִם יִגְּשׁוּ,
וְעָמְדוּ לִבְלִי־נוֹעַ.
וְאֵין אוֹת אִם חַיִּים הֵם אוֹ אִם יְרוּיִים.

אָז תִּשְׁאַל הָאֻמָּה שְׁטוּפַת דֶּמַע־וָקֶסֶם,
וְאָמְרָה: מִי אַתֶּם? וְהַשְּׁנַיִם, שׁוֹקְטִים,
יַעֲנוּ לָהּ: אֲנַחְנוּ מַגֵּשׁ הַכֶּסֶף
שֶׁעָלָיו לָךְ נִתְּנָה מְדִינַת־הַיְּהוּדִים.

כָּךְ יֹאמְרוּ. וְנָפְלוּ לְרַגְלָהּ עוֹטְפֵי־צֵל.
וְהַשְּׁאָר יְסֻפַּר בְּתוֹלְדוֹת יִשְׂרָאֵל.

Song of the Homeland

On the mountains the sun already blazes
And in the valley the dew still shines
We love you, homeland,[1]
With joy, with song and with toil.[2]
From the slopes of Lebanon to the Dead Sea
We shall crisscross you with ploughs
We shall yet cultivate and build you
We shall yet beautify you.

We will dress you in a gown of concrete and cement[3]
And lay for you a carpet of gardens,
On the soils of your redeemed fields
The harvest will chime with bells.

The poem frames the national collective saga in the metaphor of a romantic relationship between a man and woman.

[1] The word *anu* is first person plural ("we") to emphasize the collective nature of the Zionist effort. The word *moledet* ("homeland") is a feminine noun derived from the verb "to give birth."

[2] Shlonsky (p. 46) used the word *amal* to denote toil, labor, effort, and travail, whereas Alterman describes *amal* as virtuous and redemptive.

[3] The "beloved" will wear a gown of "concrete and cement," i.e., new towns and settlements.

שִׁיר מוֹלֶדֶת

בֶּהָרִים כְּבָר הַשֶּׁמֶשׁ מְלַהֶטֶת,
וּבָעֵמֶק עוֹד נוֹצֵץ הַטַּל,
אָנוּ אוֹהֲבִים אוֹתָךְ, מוֹלֶדֶת,
בְּשִׂמְחָה, בְּשִׁיר וּבֶעָמָל.

מִמּוֹרְדוֹת הַלְּבָנוֹן עַד יָם הַמֶּלַח
נַעֲבֹר אוֹתָךְ בְּמַחֲרֵשׁוֹת,
אָנוּ עוֹד נִטַּע לָךְ וְנִבְנֶה לָךְ,
אָנוּ נְיַפֶּה אוֹתָךְ מְאֹד.

נַלְבִּישֵׁךְ שַׂלְמַת בֶּטוֹן וָמֶלֶט
וְנִפְרֹשׂ לָךְ מַרְבַדֵּי גַּנִּים,
עַל אַדְמַת שְׂדוֹתַיִךְ הַנִּגְאֶלֶת
הַדָּגָן יַרְנִין פַּעֲמוֹנִים.

The desert wilderness, we will cross,
The swamps, we will drain.[5]
What we give is for your glory and satisfaction.
What has not yet been given, we shall give.

In the hills, in the hills our light shined,
We will climb the mountain.
We will leave yesterday behind,
Although the path to tomorrow remains long.

Even if the difficult path is treacherous
And even if some of us may fall,
We will love you, our homeland, forever,
We are yours in battle and in toil.

Translated by Gil Troy

[5] In pre- and post-State Israel, draining the swamps was viewed as a prominent exemplar of the Zionist mission.

הַמִּדְבָּר, אָנוּ דֶּרֶךְ בּוֹ נַחְצָבָה,
הַבִּצּוֹת, אֲנַחְנוּ נִיבַּשְׁן,
מַה נִּתֵּן לָךְ עוֹד לְהוֹד וָשֹׂבַע,
מַה עוֹד לֹא נָתַנּוּ וְנִתֵּן.

בֶּהָרִים, בֶּהָרִים זָרַח אוֹרֵנוּ,
אָנוּ נַעְפִּילָה אֶל הָהָר,
נִשְׁאַר מֵאֲחוֹרֵינוּ הָאֶתְמוֹל
אַךְ רַבָּה הַדֶּרֶךְ לַמָּחָר.

אִם קָשָׁה הִיא הַדֶּרֶךְ וּבוֹגֶדֶת,
אִם גַּם לֹא אֶחָד יִפֹּל חָלָל,
עַד עוֹלָם נֹאהַב אוֹתָךְ מוֹלֶדֶת,
אָנוּ לָךְ בַּקְּרָב וּבֶעָמָל!

Lea Goldberg

(1911–1970)

Lea Goldberg was born in Königsberg, East Russia and grew up in Kovno Lithuania. She began writing Hebrew poetry as an 11-year-old schoolgirl. Goldberg knew seven languages, studied at the Universities of Kovno, Bonn, and Berlin, and in 1933 received a PhD in Semitic Studies. Goldberg settled in Tel Aviv in 1935 and became one of Israel's leading poets, literary critics, intellectuals, and academics. Her writings include lyrical poetry, literary criticism, children books, and translations of European literature into Hebrew. Her poetry generally did not deal with political topics, but rather with personal themes and issues—childhood, love, loneliness, aging, and death.

At her funeral, the philosopher and Kabbalah scholar Gershom Scholem described her as "a paradigm of nobility," who possessed in poetry and in life an abstract "moody lyricism" that, when wedded to her "power of concrete, unencumbered expression," won her a place as one of the great poets of modern Hebrew literature.

Tel Aviv 1935

The roof-poles in those days
were like the masts of Columbus,
every crow on their pinnacles
announcing new shores.[1]

Along the streets strolled knapsacks,
and the words of a foreign country[2]
plunged into *khamsin* days[3]
like the cold blade of a knife.

How could the small air support
so many recollections
of childhood and of withered loves
and rooms grown empty elsewhere?

In 1935, Lea Goldberg emigrated to Palestine and lived in Tel Aviv. *Tel Aviv* was the Hebrew title of Theodor Herzl's book *Altneuland* ("Old New Land"). A *tel* is an artificial mound formed from the accumulated refuse of generations of people living on the same site for hundreds or thousands of years and *aviv* means "spring."

[1] To Goldberg, Tel Aviv was not a familiar location, but rather a foreign continent.

[2] Founded in 1909 by Jews as a modern housing estate on the outskirts of the ancient city port of Jaffa, Tel Aviv was dubbed "The First Hebrew City." Tel Aviv was populated by many immigrants of the First and Second Aliyah, who came from Eastern Europe, Yemen, and the Russian Empire. During the 1930s, owing to an influx of European refugees, many different languages were spoken in Tel Aviv.

[3] The word *khamsin* derives from an Arabic word "imported" into Hebrew during the British Mandate (most likely by British soldiers who served in Egypt) to describe a dry, hot, sandy, local wind affecting the entire Mediterranean basin.

תֵּל אָבִיב 1935

אָז הָיוּ הַבָּתִּים גַּגּוֹת עַל הַתְּרָנִים
שֶׁל קוֹלוּמְבּוּס סְפִינָתוֹ סְפַרְנֵי כְּתָרְנֵי
מָדָם חָד עַל שֶׁעָמַד עוֹרֵב וְכָל
אַחֶרֶת. יַבֶּשֶׁת שֶׁר בֵּשׂ

הַנּוֹסְעִים צְקָלוֹנֵי בָּרְחוֹב כָּלְכוּ וְהָלְכוּ
זָרָה אֶרֶץ שֶׁל הַשָּׂפָה וְשָׂפָה
הַחַמְסִין בְּיוֹם נִגְלֶצֶת הָיְתָה
קָרָה. סַכִּין סַב הַבְ כְּלַ

הַקְּטַנָּה הָעִיר שֶׁל הָאֲוִיר יָכוֹל אֵיךְ
הַרְבֵּה כָּךְ כָּל לְשֵׂאת
שֶׁנָּשְׁרוּ, אֲהָבוֹת יַלְדוּת, זִכְרוֹנוֹת
אֵי־בָזֶה? שֶׁרוֹקְנוּ חֲדָרִים

Like blackening snaps in a camera,
their images reversed:
white winter nights across the sea,
rainy nights of summer,
capitals dark at dawn.

Behind you foreign footsteps drummed
the marching songs of an army,
and on the sea you thought you saw
the church of your old town floating.[4]

Translated by Robert Friend

[4] Before Goldberg emigrated to Palestine, she lived in Europe where churches were prominent in both urban and rural communities.

כִּתְמוּנוֹת מַשְׁחִירוֹת בְּתוֹךְ מַצְלֵמָה
הִתְהַפְּכוּ לֵילוֹת חֹרֶף זַכִּים,
לֵילוֹת קַיִץ גְּשׁוּמִים שֶׁמֵּעֵבֶר לַיָּם
וּבְקָרִים אֲפֵלִים שֶׁל בִּירוֹת.

וְקוֹל צַעַד תּוֹפֵף אַחֲרֵי גַּבֵּךְ
שִׁירֵי לֶכֶת שֶׁל צְבָא נֵכָר,
וְנִדְמֶה־אַךְ תַּחְזִיר אֶת רֹאשֵׁךְ וּבַיָּם
שָׁטָה כְּנֵסִיַּת עִירֵךְ.

Toward Myself

The years have made up my face
with memories of love,
adorned my head
with silver threads
and made me beautiful.

Landscapes are reflected
in my eyes,
the paths I trod
have taught me to walk upright
with beautiful, though tired steps.

If you should see me now,
you would not recognise
the yesterdays you knew.
I go toward myself with a face
and looked for in vain
when I went toward you.

Translated by Robert Friend

אֵלַי

הַשָּׁנִים פִּרְכְּסוּ אֶת פָּנַי
בְּזִכְרוֹן אֲהָבוֹת
וְעָנְדוּ לְרֹאשִׁי חוּטֵי כֶּסֶף קַלִּים
עַד יָפִיתִי מְאֹד.

בְּעֵינַי נִשְׁקָפִים
הַנּוֹפִים.
וּדְרָכִים שֶׁעָבַרְתִּי
יִשְׁרוּ צְעָדַי —
עֲיֵפִים וְיָפִים.

אִם תִּרְאֵנִי עַכְשָׁו
לֹא תַכִּיר אֶת תְּמוֹלֵךְ —
אֲנִי הוֹלֶכֶת אֵלַי
בְּפָנִים שֶׁבִּקַּשְׁתָּ לַשָּׁוְא
כְּשֶׁהָלַכְתִּי אֵלֶיךָ.

"A god once commanded us…"

To the soul of Nadia

A god once commanded us to stand strong[1]
under the terrible tree of life.
And in the black wind of the years we stood,
stricken with expectation—
perhaps the fruit would fall at our feet.
But nothing happened.

And on the day of secret reckoning[2]
between him and us
we saw a hunched landscape, brown leaves falling.
and felt on our faces
a cold wind blowing.

Then said a Voice: this is your day of freedom.[3]
This is everything. And this is good.

Now towards the flame of cutting cold, alone,
I take
a few steps only
until I meet
that flickering lantern
at the corner of the street.

Translated by Robert Friend

[1] The Hebrew says *ha'el*. Since there are no capital letters in Hebrew, it is unclear whether Goldberg is referring to the word for a divinity (a "god") or The Divinity—which might be suggested by the letter *heh* (the definite article) but in terms of the poem's overall theme, it would seem unlikely. There are in fact distinct and totally contradictory translations of this poem, depending on how one interprets this key word.

פַּעַם צִוָּנוּ הָאֵל

לנשמת נדיה

פַּעַם צִוָּנוּ הָאֵל לַעֲמֹד אֵיתָנִים
מִתַּחַת לְעֵץ־הַחַיִּים הַנּוֹרָא.
וְעָמַדְנוּ מְכֵּי־צִפִּיָּה בְּרוּחַ שְׁחוֹרָה שֶׁל שָׁנִים –
אוּלַי יִפֹּל לְרַגְלֵינוּ הַפְּרִי?
וְדָבָר לֹא קָרָה.

וּבְהַגִּיעַ הַיּוֹם שֶׁל חֶשְׁבּוֹן הַסְּתָרִים
שֶׁבֵּינוּ וּבֵינֵינוּ
רָאִינוּ נוֹף כָּפוּף וְעָלִים חוּמִים נוֹשְׁרִים
וְהָרוּחַ עוֹדֶנָּה נוֹשֶׁבֶת לְעֵבֶר פָּנֵינוּ.

אָז אָמְרָה בַּת־הַקּוֹל: זֶהוּ יוֹם חֵרוּתֶךָ,
זֶה הַכֹּל. וְזֶה טוֹב.

וָאֵלֵךְ לְבַדִּי אֶל מוּל לַהַב הַקֹּר הַחוֹתֵךְ
רַק כַּמָּה צְעָדִים
עַד אוֹתוֹ הַפָּנָס הַדּוֹעֵךְ
שֶׁבְּקֶרֶן הָרְחוֹב.

---

[2] *Yom Kippur*, also known as the Day of Atonement or the "Day of Reckoning," is often described as the holiest day of the Jewish calendar. Its central themes are atonement and judgement. Jews traditionally observe this day with a 25-hour period of fasting and intensive prayer, often spending most of the day in synagogue services.

[3] Goldberg uses the word *bat kol* which is traditionally linked to God's voice and will.

Once again, the question of whether to capitalize these two words in English as "Holy Voice" or to write it as "voice" is in the eyes of the translator.

Naomi Shemer

(1930–2004)

Naomi Shemer was a popular Israeli songwriter and musician. In addition to her own writing, she set famous Hebrew poems—such as the poetry of Rahel—to music, as well as translating English poems and songs into Hebrew such as the Beatles' song, "Let it Be" (*Lu Yehi*). In May 1967, in the tense month before the outbreak of the Six-Day War between Israel, Egypt, Jordan and Syria, Shemer composed the song *Yerushalayim shel Zahav* for the annual Israel Song Festival. After the war in which the Old City of Jerusalem became part of Israeli Jerusalem, "Jerusalem of Gold" emerged as one Israel's most beloved patriotic songs, and there were even efforts to establish it as the national anthem of Israel. Naomi Shemer is buried in Kibbutz Kinneret, where she was born, and her grave is not far from that of Rahel the Poet on the shore of the Sea of Galilee.

Yerushalayim Shel Zahav

As clear as wine the wind is flying
Among the dreamy pines
As evening light is slowly dying
And a lonely bell still chimes
So many songs, so many stories
The stony hills recall...
Around her heart my city carries
A lonely ancient wall.[1]

> Yerushalayim all of gold
> Yerushalayim, bronze and light
> Within my heart I shall treasure
> Your song and sight.

Alas, the drying wells and fountains,
Forgotten market-day
The sound of horn from Temple's mountain
No longer calls to pray
The rocky caves at night are haunted
By sounds of long ago
When we were going to the Jordan
By way of Jericho.

Yerushalayim shel zahav means Jerusalem of gold, which is a reference to a special piece of jewelry mentioned in a Talmudic legend about Rabbi Akiva. Rabbi Akiva lived in poverty in a hayloft with his beloved wife Rachel, who had been disowned by her father. As he plucked the hay out of her hair in the mornings, he promised her that one day he would become wealthy and buy her a most precious piece of jewelry, the crown called, "Jerusalem of Gold," which was a golden tiara shaped like the walls of Jerusalem.

[1] "How she sits alone, the city once great with people..." (Lamentations 1:1)

יְרוּשָׁלַיִם שֶׁל זָהָב

אֲוִיר־הָרִים צָלוּל כַּיַּיִן
וְרֵיחַ אֳרָנִים
נִשָּׂא בְּרוּחַ הָעַרְבַּיִם
עִם קוֹל פַּעֲמוֹנִים

וּבְתַרְדֵּמַת אִילָן וָאֶבֶן
שְׁבוּיָה בַּחֲלוֹמָהּ
הָעִיר אֲשֶׁר בָּדָד יוֹשֶׁבֶת
וּבְלִבָּהּ חוֹמָה

יְרוּשָׁלַיִם שֶׁל זָהָב
וְשֶׁל נְחֹשֶׁת וְשֶׁל אוֹר
הֲלֹא לְכָל שִׁירַיִךְ
אֲנִי כִּנּוֹר
יְרוּשָׁלַיִם שֶׁל זָהָב
וְשֶׁל נְחֹשֶׁת וְשֶׁל אוֹר
הֲלֹא לְכָל שִׁירַיִךְ
אֲנִי כִּנּוֹר

אֵיכָה יָבְשׁוּ בּוֹרוֹת־הַמַּיִם
כִּכַּר־הַשּׁוּק רֵיקָה
וְאֵין פּוֹקֵד אֶת הַר־הַבַּיִת
בָּעִיר הָעַתִּיקָה.

וּבַמְּעָרוֹת אֲשֶׁר בַּסֶּלַע
מְיַלְּלוֹת רוּחוֹת
וְאֵין יוֹרֵד אֶל יַם־הַמֶּלַח
בְּדֶרֶךְ יְרִיחוֹ.

Yerushalayim all of gold…

But when I come to count your praises
And sing Hallel to you
With pretty rhymes I dare not crown you
As other poets do
Upon my lips is always burning
Your name, so dear, so old:
If I forgot Yerushalayim
Of bronze and light and gold…

Yerushalayim all of gold…

Back to the wells and to the fountains
Within the ancient walls
The sound of horn from Temple mountain
Loudly and proudly calls[2]
From rocky caves, this very morning
A thousand suns will glow
As we shall go down to the Jordan
By way of Jericho.

Yerushalayim all of gold…

Translated by Naomi Shemer

[2] Shemer added these lines upon hearing that Israeli soldiers had reached the Western Wall during the Six-Day War.

יְרוּשָׁלַיִם שֶׁל זָהָב...

אַךְ בְּבוֹאִי הַיּוֹם לָשִׁיר לָךְ
וְלָךְ לִקְשֹׁר כְּתָרִים
קָטֹנְתִּי מִצְּעִיר בָּנַיִךְ
וּמֵאַחֲרוֹן הַמְשׁוֹרְרִים.

כִּי שְׁמֵךְ צוֹרֵב אֶת הַשְּׂפָתַיִם
כִּנְשִׁיקַת־שָׂרָף
אִם אֶשְׁכָּחֵךְ יְרוּשָׁלַיִם
אֲשֶׁר כֻּלָּהּ זָהָב.

יְרוּשָׁלַיִם שֶׁל זָהָב...

חָזַרְנוּ אֶל בּוֹרוֹת־הַמַּיִם
לַשּׁוּק וְלַכִּכָּר
שׁוֹפָר קוֹרֵא בְּהַר־הַבַּיִת
בָּעִיר הָעַתִּיקָה.

וּבַמְּעָרוֹת אֲשֶׁר בַּסֶּלַע
אַלְפֵי שְׁמָשׁוֹת זוֹרְחוֹת –
נָשׁוּב נֵרֵד אֶל יַם הַמֶּלַח
בְּדֶרֶךְ יְרִיחוֹ!

יְרוּשָׁלַיִם שֶׁל זָהָב...

Chaim Guri

(1923–2018)

The parents of Chaim Guri (born Gurfinkel) emigrated from Russia to Palestine in 1919, where he was born in 1923. After studying at the Kadoorie Agricultural High School, he joined and served in the Palmach, the strike force of the Haganah. In 1947, he was sent to Hungary to bring Holocaust survivors to Mandate Palestine. During the 1948 Arab-Israeli War, he served as a deputy company commander in the Palmach's Negev Brigade. Guri studied literature at the Hebrew University of Jerusalem and the Sorbonne in Paris. In 1961, as a journalist, he covered the trial of Adolf Eichmann in Jerusalem. In his early years, Guri was drawn to the works of Hebrew poets such as Yonatan Ratosh, Uri Zvi Grinberg, and, especially, Nathan Alterman. Later influences included modern Russian and French poetry. Guri's poetry is a blend of the collective and the intensely personal, while the tone is often a mixture of the archaic and the colloquial. His poems are rich in biblical allusion and lyrical in nature, infused with a resonance of reflection and reminiscence.

Bab el Wad

Here I'm passing by. I stand beside the rock,
A black asphalt highway, mountain ridges, stones.
Evening darkens slowly and a sea breeze blows.
Over Beit Mahsir,[1] the first starlight glows.

Bab el Wad,
Remember our names for all time.
Where convoys to the city broke through
Our dead lie sprawled by the roadside.
The iron skeleton, like my comrade, is mute.

Here tar and lead baked in the sun
Here nights passed with fire and blades
Here grief and glory dwell side by side
A scorched armored car and unknown men's names.

Bab el Wad...

The Arabic words *Bab el Wad*—the "gate of the valley" in English and *sha'ar hagai* in Hebrew—refers to a location 23 kilometers (approximately 14 miles) from present-day Jerusalem on the Tel Aviv-Jerusalem highway where the plains meet the Judean hills. This place was the site of some of the most difficult battles of the war during its first stage, from the UN vote in November 1947 until Israel's declaration of its independence in May 1948, during which local Arab militias attempted to bar Jewish vehicles from passing through the topographic gate of the valley leading to Jerusalem.

To this day, remnants of the armored cars of the *Palmach* fighters can be seen along the highway as a memorial to those battles.

This poem was set to music in a haunting melody, most famously sung by Shoshana Damari, and it accompanies ceremonies for Yom Hazikaron, the annual Memorial Day for fallen soldiers, which is observed the day before Israel's Independence Day.

[1] *Beit Mahsir* was a Palestinian village that today is the religious moshav, *Beit Meir*.

בָּאב אֶל וָואד

פֹּה אֲנִי עוֹבֵר. נִצָּב לְיַד הָאֶבֶן.
כְּבִישׁ אַסְפַלְט שָׁחֹר, סְלָעִים וּרְכָסִים.
עֶרֶב אַט יוֹרֵד, רוּחַ יָם נוֹשֶׁבֶת
אוֹר כּוֹכָב רִאשׁוֹן מֵעֵבֶר בֵּית־מַחְסִיר.

בָּאב אֶל וָואד,
לָנֶצַח זְכֹר נָא אֶת שְׁמוֹתֵינוּ,
שַׁיָּרוֹת פָּרְצוּ בַּדֶּרֶךְ אֶל הָעִיר.
בְּצִדֵּי הַדֶּרֶךְ מֻטָּלִים מֵתֵינוּ.
שֶׁלֶד הַבַּרְזֶל שׁוֹתֵק, כְּמוֹ רֵעִי.

פֹּה רָתְחוּ בַּשֶּׁמֶשׁ זֶפֶת וְעוֹפֶרֶת.
פֹּה עָבְרוּ לֵילוֹת בְּאֵשׁ וְסַכִּינִים.
פֹּה שׁוֹכְנִים בְּיַחַד עֶצֶב וְתִפְאֶרֶת,
מִשְׁרְיָן חָרוּךְ וְשֵׁם שֶׁל אַלְמוֹנִים.

בָּאב אֶל וָואד...

And here I walk by, making no sound
And I remember them all, remember each one.
Here together we fought on cliffs and harsh ground
Here as one family, each to each bound.

Bab el Wad...

A spring day will come and cyclamens bloom
Anemones redden the hilltop and slope.
You who will walk here, on the path that we trod
Never forget us – we are Bab el Wad.

Bab el Wad...

Translated by Vivian Eden

וַאֲנִי הוֹלֵךְ, עוֹבֵר כָּאן חֶרֶשׁ חֶרֶשׁ
וַאֲנִי זוֹכֵר אוֹתָם אֶחָד אֶחָד.
כָּאן לָחַמְנוּ יַחַד עַל צוּקִים וָטֶרֶשׁ
כָּאן הָיִינוּ יַחַד מִשְׁפָּחָה אַחַת.

בָּאב אֶל וָואד...

יוֹם אָבִיב יָבוֹא וְרַקָּפוֹת תִּפְרַחְנָה,
אֹדֶם כַּלָּנִית בָּהָר וּבַמּוֹרָד.
זֶה אֲשֶׁר יֵלֵךְ בַּדֶּרֶךְ שֶׁהָלַכְנוּ
אַל יִשְׁכַּח אוֹתָנוּ, אוֹתָנוּ בָּאב אֶל וָואד.

בָּאב אֶל וָואד...

Inheritance

The ram came last.[1]
And Abraham did not know
it was the answer to the boy's question,
the boy, first issue of his vigor in the twilight of his life.

He lifted his hoary head.
When he saw it was no dream and the angel stood there—
the knife slipped from his hand.

The boy unbound
saw his father's back.

Isaac, we're told, was not offered up in sacrifice.
He lived long,
enjoyed his life, until the light of his eyes grew dim.

But he bequeathed that hour to his progeny.
They are born
with a knife in their heart.

Translated by Stanley F. Chyet

Earlier writings of Chaim Guri extolled the courage and valor of the pre-state pioneers. In later writings, Guri was to question many of the policies and practices of the newly-created State.

[1] Guri begins the poem with a reply to Isaac's question in the story of the binding of Isaac: "And Isaac said to Abraham his father, 'Father!' and he said, 'Here I am, my son.' And he said, 'Here is the fire and the wood but where is the sheep for the offering?'" (Genesis 22:7)

יְרֻשָׁה

הָאַיִל בָּא אַחֲרוֹן.
וְלֹא יָדַע עֵבְרָהָם כִּי הוּא מֵשִׁיב לִשְׁאֵלַת הַיֶּלֶד,
מֵשִׁיב לִשְׁאֵלַת הַיֶּלֶד,
רֵאשִׁיתֹ־אוֹנוֹ בְּעֵת זִקְנוֹ יוֹמוֹ עָרָב.

נָשָׂא רֹאשׁוּ אֹ הַשָׂיבַ.
בִּרְאוֹתוֹ כִּי לֹא חָלַם חֲלוֹם מוֹ
וְהַמַּלְאָךְ נִצָּב –
נָשְׁרָה הַמַּאֲכֶלֶת מִיָּדוֹ.

הַיֶּלֶד שֶׁהֻתַּר מֵאֵסוּרָיו
רָאָה אֶת גַּב אָבִיו.

יִצְחָק, כַּמְסֻפָּר, לֹא הֹעֲלָה קָרְבָּן.
הוּא חַי יָמִים רַבִּים,
רָאָה בַּטוֹב, עַד אוֹר עֵינָיו כָּהָה.

אֲבָל אֶת הַשָׁעָה הַהִיא הוֹרִישׁ לְצֶאֱצָאָיו,
הֵם נוֹלָדִים
וּמַאֲכֶלֶת בְּלִבָּם.

ISRAEL: VOICES FROM WITHIN

Section 3

Statehood
The Emergence of *Israeli* Poetry

The establishment of the State of Israel in 1948 is regarded as one of the most significant events in the history of the Jewish people. This event also resulted in a host of challenges and scenarios never before experienced by the Jewish people. Surrounded by enemies and operating under the encroaching shadow of forthcoming wars, the leadership of the new state had to assume responsibility for governing a modern democratic state; cultivating economic development and stability; and absorbing waves of Jewish immigration, mostly from the Middle East, as the population doubled within its first three-and-a-half years of existence.

In this era, particularly during the massive immigrations of the 1950s, an already emergent Hebrew linguistic dynamic became mainstream. Hebrew as *langue* (the written word of thousands of years of holy writings and liturgy) was transformed into *parole* (the spoken words of the street and daily life). This "new Hebrew," while incorporating much classical terminology, became a language of daily life, influenced by words, phrases, and cadences borrowed from Arabic, English, German, Yiddish, Russian, and the Hebrew of Sephardic and Middle-Eastern immigrants. The Yiddish word *puntchermacher* became the accepted term for one who fixes flat tires. The Arabic *inshallah* became a way of saying "hopefully" or "may it be so!" and the American English "windshield wiper," became *visher* in Hebrew. An emergent group of poets in the post-state period (e.g., Yehuda Amichai, Dalia Ravikovitch, Nathan Zach) proposed and actually did replace the poetry of pathos, historic suffering, and national renewal with a poetry of the here and now; a poetry that probes the highs and lows of love, daily pleasures and problems, and the great ambiguities of life.

Moreover, throughout the history of the new state from its creation until today the ongoing conflicts between Israel and its neighbors has remained both a covert and overt *leitmotif* of contemporary Israeli poetry. We see this phenomenon as another piece of evidence that points to the shift from poetry of pathos to poetry of vernacular.

The central poetic figure of this new era—and perhaps of all of contemporary Hebrew poetry—was the writer and poet Yehuda Amichai. His poetry, described by one of his translators as a "vernacular revolution," reflects a new language—a conversational tongue, laced with references and nuances of the Jewish past and its literature. He painted artful and personal pictures: stories of children playing and dreaming, human fallibility, flawed and fleeting love, longed-for places, the dreadful reality of war, and the yearning for a peace that might come "like wildflowers, suddenly, because the field must have it." His work, touching on seemingly small but existentially great issues, reflects a unique synthesis of accessible conversational Hebrew, traditional references and rituals, the rigors and routines of daily life, and a style often suggestive of contemporary English poetry. Moreover, Amichai pursued his writing with a modest and understated presence. He could be seen walking through Jerusalem's streets on his way back from the *shuk* (market) carrying fruits and vegetables for his family. While many regarded him as a Bialik-like figure—as the "Poet of Jerusalem" or the "Poet of Israel"—he was said to have replied: "I am just a poet."[1] Indeed, the poetry of Amichai and his colleagues can be regarded as the transformation of the Hebrew language into a spoken and varied tongue, which reflected the lives of its citizens in the 20th century state of Jews—and non-Jews—from strikingly diverse places and cultures.

---

[1] Robert Alter, *The Poetry of Yehuda Amichai*, (New York: Farrar, Strauss, and Giroux, 2015) xvii.

Nathan Zach

(1930–)

Nathan Zach was born in Germany and immigrated to Palestine in 1935. He was a key figure in the emergence of contemporary Israeli poetry as an editor, critic, translator, and poet. The *Likrat* group of poets (Zach, Amichai, Avidan) produced a new genre of Hebrew poetry, which rebelled against the lyrical pathos of pre-state poetics (as typified by Alterman and others) and called for a new poetic credo defined by contemporary themes and novel conceptions of rhyme and meter. From 1968–1979, Zach lived in England, where he received his PhD. He was awarded the Bialik Prize and the Israel Prize, among many other honors. His impact as a writer, theorist, and critic has been a shaping—and, at times, divisive—force in the Israeli literary scene and continues to be so to this day.

Confession: Refined

I was born to be refined.
Fact: I have fine hair. Want to check? Please,
here's my shampooed head bared to you. Do forgive
the little bald spots. It's just
the teeth of time.

I was born to be refined. By chance
my parents decided they needed to immigrate
to an unrefined country. It wasn't a hasty decision,
they consulted everyone they could. Even Hitler
thought it was good, definitely a sensible decision.

Thus a person born to be refined
arrived in an unrefined country.[1] You tell me
what alternative I had. I am refined, comb my hair
with a fine-toothed comb, brush my teeth, grow bald, take clothes
to the laundry, don't insult the neighbors unless
there's no alternative.

[1] Israel was often portrayed as the land of strong defiant not-so-gentle *sabras*, a cactus fruit
which is hard and prickly on the outside and soft within.

וידוי: עדין

נוֹלַדְתִּי לִהְיוֹת עָדִין.
עֻבְדָּה: יֵשׁ לִי שְׂעָרוֹת עֲדִינוֹת.
אַתֶּם רוֹצִים לִבְדֹק? בְּבַקָּשָׁה,
רֹאשִׁי הֶחָפוּף חָשׂוּף לִפְנֵיכֶם. אָנָא סְלְחוּ
עַל הַקָּרַחַת הַקְּטַנּוֹת. זֶה רַק
שִׁנֵּי הַזְּמַן.

נוֹלַדְתִּי לִהְיוֹת עָדִין. בְּמִקְרֶה
הֶחְלִיטוּ הוֹרַי שֶׁהֵם צְרִיכִים לְהַגֵּר
לְאֶרֶץ לֹא עֲדִינָה. הֵם לֹא הֶחְלִיטוּ בִּפְזִיזוּת,
הִתְיָעֲצוּ עִם כָּל מִי שֶׁיָּכְלוּ. אֲפִלּוּ הִיטְלֶר תָּמַךְ בַּהַחְלָטָה,
אָמַר שֶׁהִיא נְבוֹנָה בְּהֶחְלֵט.

כָּךְ הִגִּיעַ מִי שֶׁנּוֹלַד לִהְיוֹת עָדִין
לְאֶרֶץ לֹא עֲדִינָה. אָמְרוּ לִי אַתֶּם
אֵיזֶה בְּרֵרוֹת הָיוּ לִי. אֲנִי עֲדַיִן מִסְתָּרֵק
בְּמַסְרֵק עָדִין, מְצַחְצֵחַ שִׁנַּיִם, מַקְרִיחַ, מוֹסֵר בְּגָדִים
לְמִכְבָּסָה, לֹא מַעֲלִיב אֶת הַשְּׁכֵנִים אֶלָּא אִם כֵּן
אֵין בְּרֵרָה.

It's all a mistake, they said, there's been
some terrible mistake here. I myself confine myself
to screaming in my sleep. In your opinion,
will this help?!
Don't make me laugh. I'm a serious person
and had not my generation cursed me, my own generation,[2]
I would give you a final answer
but maybe not so very refined.

Translated by Vivian Eden

[2] The literal translation is: "If I was not cursed by my generation." Zach's group of poets criticized the poetry of the founding generation for serving the national narrative of the collective and not giving space to the voice of the individual.

הַכֹּל טָעוּת, אָמְרוּ, נָפְלָה כָּאן אֵיזוֹ טָעוּת נוֹרָאָה. אֲנִי עַצְמִי
מִסְתַּפֵּק בְּכָךְ שֶׁאֲנִי צוֹעֵק בִּשְׁנָתִי. מַה דַּעְתְּכֶם,
זֶה יַעֲזֹר?!
אַל תַּצְחִיקוּ אוֹתִי. אֲנִי בֶּן־אָדָם רְצִינִי
וְאִלְמָלֵא קִלֵּל אוֹתִי הַדּוֹר, וְהַכַּוָּנָה לְדוֹרִי,
הָיִיתִי עוֹנֶה לָכֶם תְּשׁוּבָה מוֹחֶצֶת
אֲבָל אוּלַי לֹא כָּל כָּךְ עֲדִינָה.

A Small Poem of the Fallen

How good it is I'm rid of you,
your moaning,
your strident demands.
the endless nagging,
the self-righteousness, cognizant
only of its own worth,
and the sanctimony
that will not stop
will not end
years after I cease to be,
years after I cease to breathe
and there's no longer anyone
I ever met in my life as a man
and no longer any woman
with whose body my body lay.

You, whose throat exalts
   the future,[1]
who asks and also answers
whose fears from the past lie
   at her feet
and whose eyes raised to
   the skies
demand consolation
shrieking for help
her steel foot trampling
all that's in her path,
all that comes her way
all her sons,
how good it is I'm rid of you,
   Homeland.

Translated by Vivian Eden

The Hebrew title uses the word *chalal* which means "space or void." *Chalalim* is the word used to denote soldiers or others whose lives were lost or who "fell" in wars or terrorist attacks. "The splendor, O Israel, on your heights lies slain, how have the warriors fallen!" (II Samuel 1:19)

[1] "Exultations of God in their throat and a double-edged sword in their hand…" (Psalms 149:6)

שיר חללים קטן

כַּמָּה טוֹב שֶׁנִּפְטַרְתִּי מִמֵּךְ,
מְטֻרְוֹתַיִךְ,
מִתְבִּיעוֹתַיִךְ הַקּוֹלָנִיּוֹת,
מִן הַהַטְרָדוֹת הַבִּלְתִּי־פוֹסְקוֹת,
הַצֶּדְקָנִית,
הַמַּכִּירָה רַק בְּעֵרֶךְ עַצְמָהּ,
הַצּוֹדֶקֶת בְּעֵינֵי עַצְמָהּ,
הַמִּצְטַדֶּקֶת,
שֶׁלֹּא פוֹסֶקֶת,
שֶׁלֹּא תֶּחְדַּל
שָׁנִים אַחֲרֵי שֶׁלֹּא אֶהְיֶה,
שָׁנִים אַחֲרֵי שֶׁלֹּא אֶחְיֶה,
כְּשֶׁלֹּא יִהְיֶה עוֹד אִיש
שֶׁהִכַּרְתִּי בְּחַיַּי כְּאִיש
הֲשֶׁה גַּם תִּהְיֶה וְלֹא
שֶׁגּוּפִי יִשְׁכַּב עִם גּוּפָהּ.

שֶׁרוֹמְמוּת הֶעָתִיד בִּגְרוֹנָהּ,
שֶׁשּׁוֹאֶלֶת וְגַם מְשִׁיבָה,
שֶׁחֲרֵדוֹת הֶעָבָר לְרַגְלֶיהָ
וְעֵינֶיהָ נְשׂוּאוֹת לַמְּרוֹמִים
בְּתָבְעָהּ מֵהֶם נִחוּמִים
בְּצָרִיחָתָהּ נוֹרָאָה לְעֶזְרָה
כְּשֶׁהִיא דּוֹרֶסֶת בְּרֶגֶל פְּלָדָה
כָּל שֶׁנִּמְצָא בְּדַרְכָּהּ,
כָּל שֶׁנִּזְדַּמֵּן אֵלֶיהָ,
כָּל שֶׁהָיָה מִבְּנֶיהָ,
כַּמָּה טוֹב שֶׁנִּפְטַרְתִּי מִמֵּךְ, מוֹלֶדֶת.

Yehuda Amichai

(1924–2000)

Yehuda Amichai was born on May 3, 1924 as Ludwig Pfeuffer in Würzburg, Germany and he Hebraized his family name to Amichai ("my people lives") in 1946. In 1935, his family moved to Palestine, where they lived an Orthodox Jewish life. While Amichai was to adopt a secular lifestyle, his poetic works reflected a rich understanding and appreciation of traditional Jewish life's texts and themes. After a few years as a teacher, Amichai published his first book of poetry in 1955 and, over time, became recognized not only as Israel's leading poet but also as a significant literary figure in 20th-century world poetry. His poems have been translated into numerous languages (including French, English, Polish, Chinese, Catalan, Japanese, and others) and he was reputed to have been nominated several times for a Nobel Prize. His unique poetic style frequently "spoke" in colloquial Hebrew and encompassed a potpourri of topics that made his poetry accessible to broad audiences. Amichai is often compared to Dylan Thomas, W.H. Auden, and William Carlos Williams, but ultimately in describing himself he would likely refer the reader to one of his poems:

"What kind of man are you?" people ask me.
I am a man with a complex network of pipes in my soul,
sophisticated machineries of emotion,
and a precisely monitored memory system
of the late twentieth century,
but with an old body from ancient days
And a God more obsolete even than my body.

– From "What Kind of Man" by Yehuda Amichai
Translated by Chana Bloch

Tourists

Visits of condolence is all we get from them.
They squat at the Holocaust Memorial,[1]
They put on grave faces at the Wailing Wall
And they laugh behind heavy curtains
In their hotels.[2]
They have their pictures taken
Together with our famous dead
At Rachel's Tomb and Herzl's Tomb
And on the top of Ammunition Hill.
They weep over our sweet boys
And lust over our tough girls
And hang up their underwear
To dry quickly
In cool, blue bathrooms.[3]

Once I sat on the steps by a gate at David's Tower, I placed my two heavy baskets at my side.[4] A group of tourists was standing around their guide and I became their target marker. "You see that man with the baskets? Just right of his head there's an arch from the Roman period. Just right of his head." "But he's moving, he's moving!" I said to myself: redemption[5] will come only if their guide tells them, "You see that arch from the Roman period? It's not important: but next to it, left and down a bit, there sits a man who's bought fruit and vegetables for his family."

Translated by Glenda Abramson & Tudor Parfitt

[1] The word *yoshvim* here translated as "squatting," literally means "sitting," which suggests the practice of "sitting *shiva*"—the seven-day mourning period.

[2] The luxurious hotels where tourists stay in Jerusalem.

[3] The trappings of modern travel.

[4] The linguistic style, spacing, and printing of the poem changes from poetry in the first section to prose in the second section.

[5] *Geula* refers to the eventual salvation of the world by God.

תַּיָּרִים

בִּקּוּרֵי אֲבֵלִים הֵם עוֹרְכִים אֶצְלֵנוּ,
יוֹשְׁבִים בְּיָד וָשֵׁם, מַרְצִינִים לְיַד הַכֹּתֶל הַמַּעֲרָבִי
וְצוֹחֲקִים מֵאֲחוֹרֵי וִילוֹנוֹת כְּבֵדִים בְּחַדְרֵי מָלוֹן,
מִצְטַלְמִים עִם מֵתִים חֲשׁוּבִים בְּקֶבֶר רָחֵל
וּבְקֶבֶר הֶרְצְל וּבַגִּבְעַת הַתַּחְמֹשֶׁת,
בּוֹכִים עַל יְפִי גְּבוּרַת נְעָרֵינוּ
וְחוֹשְׁקִים בְּקַשְׁיחוּת נַעֲרוֹתֵינוּ
וְתוֹלִים אֶת תַּחְתּוֹנֵיהֶם
לְיִבּוּשׁ מָהִיר
בְּאַמְבַּטְיָה כְּחֻלָּה וְצוֹנֶנֶת.

פַּעַם יָשַׁבְתִּי עַל מַדְרֵגוֹת לְיַד שַׁעַר בִּמְצוּדַת דָּוִד, אֶת שְׁנֵי הַסַּלִּים הַכְּבֵדִים שַׂמְתִּי לְיָדִי. עָמְדָה שָׁם קְבוּצַת תַּיָּרִים סְבִיב הַמַּדְרִיךְ וְשִׁמַּשְׁתִּי לָהֶם נְקֻדַּת צִיּוּן. "אַתֶּם רוֹאִים אֶת הָאִישׁ הַזֶּה עִם הַסַּלִּים? קְצָת יָמִינָה מֵרֹאשׁוֹ נִמְצֵאת קֶשֶׁת מִן הַתְּקוּפָה הָרוֹמִית. קְצָת יָמִינָה מֵרֹאשׁוֹ". אֲבָל הוּא זָז, הוּא זָז! אָמַרְתִּי בְּלִבִּי: הַגְּאֻלָּה תָּבוֹא רַק אִם יַגִּידוּ לָהֶם: אַתֶּם רוֹאִים שָׁם אֶת הַקֶּשֶׁת מִן הַתְּקוּפָה הָרוֹמִית? לֹא חָשׁוּב: אֲבָל לְיָדָהּ, קְצָת שְׂמֹאלָה וּלְמַטָּה מִמֶּנָּה, יוֹשֵׁב אָדָם שֶׁקָּנָה פֵּרוֹת וִירָקוֹת לְבֵיתוֹ.

And the Child Is No More

My son, again you worry me.
From time to time you worry me,
so regularly it should calm me.

I remember once, when you were little,
we saw a fire together in a big hotel.
The flames and the water and the smoke,
the wailing and the shouting and the madly flashing lights,
all these saved me from lots of talk
on what life is. And we stood in silence.

I ask myself where my father hid his fear,
perhaps in a closed closet
or some other place beyond the reach of children,
perhaps deep in his heart.

But now again you worry me.
I'm always looking for you,
this time among the mists of the Upper Galilee.[1]
I am a mist father.
And the child is no more, for he is already grown.

Translated by Robert Alter

The title begins with the letter *vav*, which in the Bible can mean either "and" or "but." This suggests that the poem may or may not be about something new. Perhaps it is merely a continuation of the long and painful story of fathers and sons, connections and separations.

[1] The Upper Galilee was one of the first regions of Jewish settlement and rebuilding of the land in the early 20th century. Despite its relatively short distance from the center of the country, the Galilee in the North and the Negev in the South were typically regarded as being on the periphery.

וְהַיֶּלֶד אֵינֶנּוּ

בְּנִי, אַתָּה שׁוּב מַדְאִיג אוֹתִי.
מִזְמַן לְזְמַן אַתָּה מַדְאִיג אוֹתִי
בָּרְבִיעוּת שֶׁהָיְתָה צְרִיכָה לְהַרְגִּיעַ אוֹתִי.

אֲנִי זוֹכֵר שֶׁפַּעַם, כְּשֶׁהָיִיתָ קָטָן,
רָאִינוּ יַחְדָּו שְׂרֵפָה בְּמָלוֹן גָּדוֹל.
הָאֵשׁ וְהַמַּיִם וְהֶעָשָׁן,
הַיְלָדוֹת וְהַצְּעָקוֹת וְהָאוֹרוֹת הַמְהַבְהֲבִים בְּטֵרוּף,
כָּל אֵלֶּה חָסְכוּ לִי הַרְבֵּה דְּבוּרִים
עַל מַה הֵם הַחַיִּים. וְעָמַדְנוּ בַּדְּמָמָה.

אֲנִי שׁוֹאֵל אֶת עַצְמִי אֵיפֹה הֶחְבִּיא אָבִי
אֶת הַפַּחַד שֶׁלּוֹ, אוּלַי בְּאָרוֹן סָגוּר
אוֹ בְּמָקוֹם אַחֵר מַחוּץ לְהֶשֵּׂג יְדֵי הַיְלָדִים
אוּלַי עָמֹק בְּלִבּוֹ.

אֲבָל עַכְשָׁו אַתָּה שׁוּב מַדְאִיג אוֹתִי.
אֲנִי מְחַפֵּשׂ אוֹתְךָ תָּמִיד,
הַפַּעַם בֵּין עַרְפִלֵּי הַגָּלִיל הָעֶלְיוֹן,
אֲנִי אַבָּא עֲרָפֶל.
וְהַיֶּלֶד אֵינֶנּוּ, כִּי הוּא כְּבָר מְבֻגָּר.

Jerusalem

On a roof in the Old City
laundry hanging in the late afternoon sunlight:
the white sheet of a woman who is my enemy,
the towel of a man who is my enemy,
to wipe off the sweat of his brow.

In the sky of the Old City
a kite.
At the other end of the string,
a child
I can't see
because of the wall.

We have put up many flags,
they have put up many flags.
To make us think that they're happy.
To make them think that we're happy.

Translated by Stephen Mitchell

יְרוּשָׁלַיִם

עַל גַּג בָּעִיר הָעַתִּיקָה,
כְּבִיסָה מוּאֶרֶת בְּאוֹר אַחֲרוֹן שֶׁל יוֹם:
תֵּבֶת שֶׁל יִן לָבָן שֶׁל דִּינָסָ,
מַגֶּבֶת שֶׁל אוֹיֵב
לְנַגֵּב בָּה אֶת זֵעַת תֹּה אַפֿו.

וּבִשְׁמֵי הָעִיר הָעַתִּיקָה
עֲפִיפוֹן.
וּבִקְצֵה הַחוּט –
יֶלֶד,
שֶׁלֹא רָאִיתִיו אוֹתוֹ,
בִּגְלַל הַחוֹמָה.

הֶעֱלֵינוּ הַרְבֵּה דְּגָלִים,
הֶעֱלוּ הַרְבֵּה דְּגָלִים.
כְּדֵי שֶׁנַּחְשֹׁב שֶׁהֵם שְׂמֵחִים.
כְּדֵי שֶׁיַּחְשְׁבוּ וּנֶאֱנַחְנוּ שְׂמֵחִים.

Instead of a love poem

To Chana

From "thou shalt not seethe a kid in its mother's milk,"[1]
They made the many laws of Kashrut,[2]
But the kid is forgotten and the milk is forgotten and
        the mother
Is forgotten.

In this way from "I love you"
We made all our life together
But I've not forgotten you
As you were then.

Translated by Glenda Abramson and Tudor Parfitt

[1] "…You shall not boil a kid in its mother's milk." (Exodus 23:19)

[2] *Kashrut* refers to the set of laws governing what is permitted and forbidden in cooking and eating according to Jewish law. In this poem, the reference is to the separation of milk and meat.

בִּמְקוֹם שִׁיר אַהֲבָה

לחנה

כְּמוֹ שֶׁמְּ"לֹא־תְבַשֵּׁל גְּדִי בַּחֲלֵב אִמּוֹ",
עָשׂוּ אֶת כָּל הַחֻקִּים הָרַבִּים שֶׁל כַּשְׁרוּת,
אֲבָל הַגְּדִי שָׁכוּחַ וְהֶחָלָב שָׁכוּחַ וְהָאֵם שְׁכוּחָה,

כָּךְ מֵ"אֲנִי אוֹהֵב אוֹתָךְ"
עָשִׂינוּ אֶת כָּל חַיֵּינוּ יַחְדָּו.
אֲבָל אֲנִי לֹא שָׁכַחְתִּי אוֹתָךְ
כְּפִי שֶׁהָיִית אָז.

Dalia Ravikovitch

(1936–2015)

Dalia Ravikovitch was born in Ramat Gan, studied at the Hebrew University of Jerusalem, and worked as a high school teacher, a journalist, a critic, and above all else, a poet. Her first book of poetry was published in 1959, at the age of 23, and its arrival marked the rise of a literary star. Although stylistically different from Zach and Amichai, she joined them as one of the new torchbearers of Israeli poetry. She also wrote three collections of short stories, two poetry books for children, and translated works ranging from T.S. Eliot's poetry to *Mary Poppins*. Her poetry has been translated into 23 languages and appears in Israeli film, theatre, dance, and art. Encompassing personal statements of loss, love, beauty, and the struggle for existence, as well as musings of national and political significance, her poetry was hailed by the Israel Prize committee in 1999 as "one of the support pillars of lyrical Hebrew verse." It combines the profane and the sacred, the ornate and the unadorned, the contemporary and the ancient. Her death shook the literary world and the general public, which had come to regard her as a contentious yet treasured poet.

Lying upon the Waters

Stinking Mediterranean city[1]
stretched out over the waters
head between her knees,[2]
her body befouled with smoke and dunghills.
Who will raise from the dunghills[3]
a rotten Mediterranean city,
her feet scabby and galled?
Her sons requite each other
with knives.[4]

Now the city is flooded with crates of plums and grapes,
cherries laid out in the marketplace
in sight of every passerby,
the setting sun peachy pink.
Who could really hate
a doped-up Mediterranean city
lowing like a cow in heat,
her walls Italian marble and crumbling sand,
decked out in rags and broidered work.
But she doesn't mean it at all,
doesn't mean anything at all.

[1] The poem would seem to be referring to Tel Aviv, Israel's major metropolis and coastal city.

[2] "And Ahab went up to eat and to drink, while Elijah had gone up to the top of Carmel and stooped to the ground and put his head between his knees." (I Kings 18:42)

[3] "He raises the poor from the dust, from the dung-heap lifts the needy." (Psalms 113:7)

[4] "How has the faithful town become a whore? Filled with justice, where righteousness did lodge, and now—murderers." (Isaiah 1:21) The reference might also be to the knives used in the *shuk*—marketplace—to cut slices of cool watermelon on hot summer days.

שוכבת על המים

עִיר יָם תִּיכוֹנִית מַסְרִיחָה
נִּהֲרָה עַל הַמַּיִם
רֹאשָׁה בֵּין בִּרְכֶּיהָ
גּוּפָה מְזֹהָם בֶּעָשָׁן וְאַשְׁפּוֹת.
מִי יָרִים מֵאַשְׁפּוֹת
עִיר יָם תִּיכוֹנִית רְקוּבָה
רַגְלֶיהָ מְכוֹת גֶּרֶב,
בָּנֶיהָ זֶה לָזֶה
גּוֹמְלִים בְּסַכִּינִים.

וְעַכְשָׁו הֵצִיפָה הָעִיר אַרְגְּזֵי עֲנָבִים וּשְׁזִיפִים
דְּבְדְּבָנִים עוֹמְדִים בַּשּׁוּק לְעֵינֵי הָעוֹבְרִים.
הַשֶּׁמֶשׁ הַשׁוֹקַעַת וְרֻדָּה כָּאֲפַרְסֵק
מִי יוּכַל לִשְׁנֹא בְּרְצִינוּת
עִיר יָם תִּיכוֹנִית מְסֻמֶּמֶת
כְּמוֹ פָּרָה גוֹעָה מְיֻחֶמֶת
כְּתָלֶיהָ שַׁיִשׁ אִיטַלְקִי עִם חוֹל יָם מִתְפּוֹרֵר.
לְבוּשָׁה סְחָבוֹת עִם רִקְמָה
אֲבָל הִיא לֹא מִתְכַּוֶּנֶת,
לֹא מִתְכַּוֶּנֶת לְשׁוּם דָּבָר.

And the sea is full, brimming at her blind forehead,
and the sun pours his horn of mercy upon her
when at dusk his wrath subsides.
And the squashes and cucumbers and lemons bursting
with color and juice
waft over her the sweet savor of summer perfumes.
And she is not worthy.
Not worthy of love or pity.

Filthy Mediterranean city
how my soul is bound up with her soul.[5]
Because of a lifetime,
an entire lifetime.[6]

Translated by Chana Bloch and Chana Kronfeld

[5] "And it happened as [David] finished speaking with Saul, that Jonathan's very self became bound up with David's, and Jonathan loved him as himself." (I Samuel 18:1)

[6] In the Hebrew Bible there are no punctuation marks. One way of emphasizing a point it to say the word twice.

וְהַיָּם מָלֵא סָמוּךְ לְמִצְחָהּ הֶעָזֹר
וְהַשֶּׁמֶשׁ שׁוֹלֵחַ אֵלֶיהָ קַרְנַיִם שׁוֹפְעוֹת רַחֲמִים
כַּאֲשֶׁר יָפוּג זַעֲמוֹ לְעֵת הַשְּׁקִיעָה.
וְהַדְּלוּעִים וְהַמְּלָפְפוֹנִים וְהַלִּימוֹנִים הַמִּתְפַּקְעִים מִצֶּבַע וּמִיץ
נוֹשְׁבִים עָלֶיהָ נִיחוֹחַ קַל שֶׁל בָּשְׂמֵי קַיִץ.
וְהִיא אֵינָהּ רְאוּיָה.
אֵינָהּ רְאוּיָה לְאַהֲבָה אוֹ לְחֶמְלָה.

עִיר יָם תִּיכוֹנִית מְזֹהֶמֶת
אֵיךְ נַפְשִׁי נִקְשָׁרָה בְּנַפְשָׁהּ.
בִּגְלַל מֶשֶׁךְ הַחַיִּים,
בִּגְלַל מֶשֶׁךְ הַחַיִּים.

Pride

Even rocks crack, I tell you,
and not on account of age.
For years they lie on their backs in the cold and the heat,
so many years,
it almost creates the impression of calm.
They don't move, so the cracks can hide.
A kind of pride.
Years pass over them as they wait.
Whoever is going to shatter them
hasn't come yet.
And so the moss flourishes, the seaweed is cast about,
the sea bursts out and slides back,
and it seems the rocks are perfectly still.
Till a little seal comes to rub against them,
comes and goes.
And suddenly the stone has an open wound.
I told you, when rocks crack, it happens by surprise.
Not to mention people.

Translated by Chana Bloch and Chana Kronfeld

גאווה

אֲפִלּוּ סְלָעִים נִשְׁבָּרִים, אֲנִי אוֹמֶרֶת לָךְ,
וְלֹא מֵחֲמַת זִקְנָה.
שָׁנִים רַבּוֹת הֵם שׁוֹכְבִים עַל גַּבָּם בַּחֹם וּבַקֹּר,
שָׁנִים כֹּה רַבּוֹת,
כִּמְעַט נוֹצָר רֹשֶׁם שֶׁל שַׁלְוָה.
אֵין הֵם זָזִים מִמְּקוֹמָם וְכָךְ נִסְתָּרִים הַבְּקִיעִים.
מֵעֵין גַּאֲוָה.
שָׁנִים רַבּוֹת עוֹבְרוֹת עֲלֵיהֶם בְּצִפִּיָּה.
מִי שֶׁעָתִיד לְשַׁבֵּר אוֹתָם
עֲדַיִן לֹא בָּא.
וְאָז הָאֵזוֹב מְשַׂגְשֵׂג, הָאַצּוֹת נִגְרָשׁוֹת וְהַיָּם מֵגִיחַ וְחוֹזֵר,
וְדוֹמֶה, הֵם לְלֹא תְּנוּעָה.
עַד שֶׁיָּבוֹא כֶּלֶב יָם קָטָן לְהִתְחַכֵּךְ עַל הַסְּלָעִים
יָבוֹא וְיֵלֵךְ.
וּפִתְאֹם הָאֶבֶן פְּצוּעָה.
אָמַרְתִּי לָךְ, כְּשֶׁסְּלָעִים נִשְׁבָּרִים זֶה קוֹרֶה בְּהַפְתָּעָה.
וּמַה גַּם אֲנָשִׁים.

Yona Wallach

(1944–1985)

Yona Wallach was part of the new generation known as "the Tel Aviv poets." She led a bold and pathbreaking campaign of feminist writing and expression, stretching the boundaries of language and propriety in her poetry. She was unique in her focus on the language of the self—physical, spiritual, mental, and erotic. The Institute for the Translation of Hebrew Literature wrote that Wallach's poetry combined "rock and roll, Jungian psychology and street slang in a body of work known for its break-neck pace and insistent sexuality." Unconfined by conventional poetic structures and by the accepted norms of the time, she established new frontiers of expression and openness in contemporary Hebrew poetry. A beautiful, haunted, and prolific poet, she became a public persona on the Israeli cultural scene before succumbing to illness at age 41.

*

And this is not what that[1]
Will satisfy
My hunger
This is not what
Will satisfy
Me[2]
No
This is not this.

Translated by Yair Mazor

[1] The language of this poem mixes everyday terms ("this is not what that") with provocative and sensual words (like "satisfy" and "hunger").

[2] The Hebrew phrase actually means "ease my mind."

*

וְזֶה לֹא מַה שֶׁ
יַשְׂבִּיעַ אֶת
רַעֲבוֹנִי לֹא
זֶה לֹא
מַה
שֶׁיַּנִּיחַ אֶת
דַּעְתִּי
לֹא
זֶה לֹא זֶה.

*

Never will I hear the sweet voice of God
Never will his voice pass beneath my window
Great drops will fall on the open plains a sign
God will not come to my window again
How might I see his sweet body again
To plunge into his eyes I'll never descend to draw forth again
Looks will change in the world like wind
How will I recall this beauty without crying
Days will pass through my life like body convulsions
By fragments of touch memories shattering still more from weeping
The shape of his movement charms the air as he moves
Never will the voice of longing pass beyond the threshold[1]
When he resurrects man like his dead with memories, like being[2]
If only his sweet look would stand by my bed and I'd cry.

Translated by Warren Bargad and Stanley Chyet

[1] Wallach presents the relationship with God in physical and even sensual terms. She, like Alterman and Goldberg, bemoans the loss of a God in whom to believe.

[2] "A time to be born and a time to die..." (Ecclesiastes 3:2)

*

לְעוֹלָם לֹא אֶשְׁמַע אֶת קוֹלוֹ הַמָּתוֹק שֶׁל הָאֱלֹהִים

לְעוֹלָם לֹא יַעֲבֹר עוֹד קוֹלוֹ תַּחַת חַלּוֹנִי

טִפּוֹת גְּדוֹלוֹת יֵרְדוּ בַּמֶּרְחָבִים אוֹת

אֵין הָאֱלֹהִים בָּא עוֹד בְּחַלּוֹנִי

אֵיךְ אוּכַל עוֹד לִרְאוֹת אֶת גּוּפוֹ הַמָּתוֹק

לְצַלֵּל בְּעֵינָיו לֹא אֶרֶד עוֹד לִשְׁלוֹת

מַבָּטִים יַחְלְפוּ בַּיְקוּם כְּמוֹ רוּחַ

אֵיךְ אֶזְכֹּר אֶת הַיְּפִי הַזֶּה וְלֹא אֹבַךְ

יָמִים יַעַבְרוּ בְּחַיַּי כְּמוֹ רְטָטִים בַּגּוּף

לְיַד רְסִיסִים שֶׁל זִכְרֵי מַגָּע נִשְׁבָּרִים עוֹד יוֹתֵר מְבֶּכֶה

מַקְסִימָה אֶת הָאֲוִיר צוּרַת תְּנוּעָתוֹ בְּנוֹעוֹ

לְעוֹלָם לֹא יַעֲבֹר קוֹל הַגַּעְגּוּעִים אֶת הַסַּף

עֵת אָדָם יְחַיֶּה כְּמוֹ מֵתָיו בִּזְכְרוֹנוֹת, כְּמוֹ הֲוָיָה

וְלוּא יַעֲמֹד מַבָּטוֹ הַמָּתוֹק לְיַד מִטָּתִי וְאֶבְכֶּה.

*

And every exhaling was Oh
And every exhaling was more Oh
And at every exhaling I turned to be Oh
And I am yes I am filled with yes
I am yes yes I am filled with yes
I am content I tend to forgive
I love I am hungry
I am yes I am filled with yes yes
And in every exhaling I was Oh
And in every exhaling I grew bigger to say Oh
Beads played with me
Bells pounded me
For a long time I have not been.

Translated by Yair Mazor

*

וְכָל נְשִׁיפָה הָיְתָה אוֹי

וְכָל נְשִׁיפָה הָיְתָה אוֹי יוֹתֵר

וּבְכָל נְשִׁיפָה הָפַכְתִּי לִהְיוֹת אוֹי

וְאוֹי כְּשֶׁהָפַכְתִּי כְּלִי לְאוֹי

וַהֲרֵי אֲנִי כֵּן אֲנִי כְּלִי כֵּן

אֲנִי כֵּן כֵּן אֲנִי מָלֵא בְּכֵן

אֲנִי מְרֻצֶּה אֲנִי סַלְחָן

אֲנִי אוֹהֵב אֲנִי רָעֵב

אֲנִי כֵּן אֲנִי מָלֵא בְּכֵן כֵּן

וּבְכָל נְשִׁיפָה הָיִיתִי אוֹי

וּבְכָל נְשִׁיפָה הִגְדַּלְתִּי אוֹי

חֲרוּזִים צִיעַצְעוּ בִּי

פַּעֲמוֹנִים הָלְמוּ אוֹתִי

כְּבָר מִזְּמַן הָיֹה הָיִיתִי

Dan Pagis

(1929–1986)

Dan Pagis was born in Radauti Bukovina, Romania and was imprisoned in a concentration camp in the Ukraine during the Second World War. He managed to escape in 1944 and arrived on the shores of Palestine two years later. He earned his PhD from the Hebrew University of Jerusalem, where he later taught medieval Jewish poetry and became one of Israel's prominent scholars of the 11th and 12th century verse of Solomon Ibn Gabirol, Moses Ibn Ezra, and Judah Halevi. He also translated many works of literature into Hebrew while writing and publishing several volumes of his own poetry.

Written in Pencil in the Sealed Boxcar

Here in this shipment[1]
I Eve
With Abel my son[2]
if you see my older son
Cain the son of Adam[3]
Tell him that I

Translated by John Felstiner

The title of this poem refers to the German railroad cars that were used as part of the mass deportation of Jews, as well as other victims of the Holocaust, to the Nazi concentration, forced labor, and extermination camps. Usually the transport of people was done in a sealed cattle car.

[1] The word *mishlo'ach* used in the poem usually refers to a package or a shipment—not to people.

[2] The story of Cain's murder of Abel and its consequences is told in Genesis 4:1–15. Cain and Abel are the first two sons of Adam and Eve. Cain, the firstborn, was a farmer and his brother, Abel, was a shepherd. The brothers each made sacrifices to God, but God favored Abel's sacrifice and rejected Cain's. Cain then murdered Abel, whereupon God punished Cain to a life of wandering.

[3] In Hebrew and Yiddish, to be a *ben adam* (son of Adam) is cognate with the German word *Mensch*, a "human being," i.e., a person of integrity and honor.

כָּתוּב בְּעִפָּרוֹן בַּקָּרוֹן הֶחָתוּם

כָּאן בַּמִּשְׁלוֹחַ הַזֶּה

אֲנִי חַוָּה

עִם הֶבֶל בְּנִי

אִם תִּרְאוּ אֶת בְּנִי הַגָּדוֹל

קַיִן בֶּן אָדָם

תַּגִּידוּ לוֹ שֶׁאֲנִי

Zelda Mishkowsky

(1916–1984)

Zelda Mishkowsky, a descendant of the Chabad Lubavitcher rabbinic dynasty, was born in the Ukraine and immigrated to Palestine at the age of 12. Popularly known by her first name, she was a pious woman who lived most of her life in Jerusalem's very religious neighborhoods, yet her poetry was admired by people across the breadth of Israeli society. Her English translator, Marcia Falk, notes that Zelda was Amos Oz's teacher in the second grade—an experience that had a profound effect on the young writer. In his memoir, Oz wrote that she was prone to grammatical error and a Hebrew that overflowed with Yiddish. But when she told a story about snow, he wrote, "it seemed written in words of snow. And when it was about fires, the words themselves burned." The hypnotic sweetness of her tales made it seem "as though the writer had dipped the letters in wine: the words went spinning in the mouth."

So too was her poetry. Influenced by religious belief, plant life, Hasidic parables, wildlife, Orthodox practice, and folklore, Zelda was one of the few poets able to traverse the divide that at times separates religious and secular society in Israel. In 1976, Zelda moved to the religious Jerusalem neighborhood of Sha'arei Hesed, which borders the mainly secular, middle-class neighborhood of Rehavia. This new locale enabled Zelda's house to become a meeting place for religious and non-religious academics, kibbutzniks, students, friends, and guests who were attracted by her warmth, wisdom, and poetry. Some of her poems were set to music, and she became, as the author Haim Be'er wrote after the publication of her first volume of poetry, a "Cinderella who has appeared from the dwellings of the ultra-Orthodox."[1]

---

[1] Yael Freund-Avraham, "Zelda: The Forgotten Poet That the Public Insisted on Remembering," Makor Rishon, July 19, 2015, www.makorrishon.co.il/nrg/online/47/ART2/710/447.html.

Light a Candle

Light a candle,
drink wine.
Softly the Sabbath has plucked
the sinking sun.
Slowly the Sabbath descends,
the rose of heaven in her hand.

How can the Sabbath
plant a huge and shining flower
in a blind and narrow heart?
How can the Sabbath
plant the bud of angels
in a heart of raving flesh?
Can the rose of immortality grow
in a generation enslaved
to destruction,
a generation enslaved
to death?

Light a candle!
Drink wine!
Slowly the Sabbath descends
and in her hand the flower,
and in her hand
the sinking sun.

Translated by Marcia Falk

הדליקו נר

הַדְלִיקוּ נֵר
שְׁתוּ יַיִן.
הַשַּׁבָּת קָטְפָה בַּלָּאט
אֶת הַשֶּׁמֶשׁ הַשּׁוֹקַעַת.
הַשַּׁבָּת יוֹרֶדֶת לְאַט
וּבְיָדָהּ שׁוֹשַׁנַּת הָרְקִיעִים.

אֵיךְ תִּשְׁתֹּל הַשַּׁבָּת
פֶּרַח עָצוּם וּמֵאִיר
בְּלֵב צַר וְעִוֵּר?
אֵיךְ תִּשְׁתֹּל הַשַּׁבָּת
אֶת צִיץ הַמַּלְאָכִים
בְּלֵב בָּשָׂר מְשֻׁגָּע וְהוֹלֵל?
הֲתִצְמַח שׁוֹשַׁנַּת הָאַלְמֶוֶת
בְּדוֹר שֶׁל עֲבָדִים
לַהֶרֶס,
בְּדוֹר שֶׁל עֲבָדִים
לַמָּוֶת?!

הַדְלִיקוּ נֵר!
שְׁתוּ יַיִן!
הַשַּׁבָּת יוֹרֶדֶת בַּלָּאט
וּבְיָדָהּ הַפֶּרַח,
וּבְיָדָהּ
הַשֶּׁמֶשׁ הַשּׁוֹקַעַת...

Each of Us Has a Name

Each of us has a name[1]
given by God
and given by our parents[2]

Each of us has a name
given by our stature and our smile
and given by what we wear

Each of us has a name
given by the mountains
and given by our walls

Each of us has a name
given by the stars[3]
and given by our neighbors

Each of us has a name
given by our sins
and given by our longing

Each of us has a name
given by our enemies
and given by our love

Each of us has a name
given by our celebrations
and given by our work

Each of us has a name
given by the seasons
and given by our blindness

Each of us has a name
given by the sea
and given by
our death.

Translated by Marcia Falk

[1] "Male and female He created them, and He blessed them and called their name humankind on the day they were created." (Genesis 5:2)

[2] "You find that a man is known by three names: the name by which his father and mother call him, the name by which other men call him, and the one he earns for himself; the most important name is the one he earns for himself." (*Midrash Tanchuma*)

[3] The word used in the poem is *mazalot*, which refers to the signs of the zodiac.

לכל איש יש שם

לְכָל אִישׁ יֵשׁ שֵׁם

שֶׁנָּתַן לוֹ אֱלֹהִים

וְנָתְנוּ לוֹ אָבִיו וְאִמּוֹ

לְכָל אִישׁ יֵשׁ שֵׁם

שֶׁנָּתְנוּ לוֹ קוֹמָתוֹ וְאֹפֶן חִיּוּכוֹ

וְנָתַן לוֹ הָאָרִיג

לְכָל אִישׁ יֵשׁ שֵׁם

שֶׁנָּתְנוּ לוֹ הֶהָרִים

וְנָתְנוּ לוֹ כְּתָלָיו

לְכָל אִישׁ יֵשׁ שֵׁם

שֶׁנָּתְנוּ לוֹ הַמַּזָּלוֹת

וְנָתְנוּ לוֹ שְׁכֵנָיו

לְכָל אִישׁ יֵשׁ שֵׁם

שֶׁנָּתְנוּ לוֹ חֲטָאָיו

וְנָתְנָה לוֹ כְּמִיהָתוֹ

לְכָל אִישׁ יֵשׁ שֵׁם

שֶׁנָּתְנוּ לוֹ שׂוֹנְאָיו

וְנָתְנָה לוֹ אַהֲבָתוֹ

לְכָל אִישׁ יֵשׁ שֵׁם

שֶׁנָּתְנוּ לוֹ חַגָּיו

וְנָתְנָה לוֹ מְלַאכְתּוֹ

לְכָל אִישׁ יֵשׁ שֵׁם

שֶׁנָּתְנוּ לוֹ תְּקוּפוֹת הַשָּׁנָה

וְנָתַן לוֹ עִוְרוֹנוֹ

לְכָל אִישׁ יֵשׁ שֵׁם

שֶׁנָּתַן לוֹ הַיָּם

וְנָתַן לוֹ

מוֹתוֹ.

Meir Wiezeltier

(1941–)

Meir Wiezeltier was born in Moscow. His father was killed while serving in the Red Army in Leningrad, so Wiezeltier, who fled Moscow for Siberia with his mother and two older sisters, never knew him. After the war, he spent two years in Poland, Germany, and France as a displaced person before immigrating with his family to Israel. Wiezeltier grew up on a kibbutz and in the coastal city of Netanya. In 1955, at the age of 14, he moved to Tel Aviv, a city where he has lived for decades. He published his first poems at the age of 18 and quickly became, by the early sixties, a central figure among the "Tel Aviv Poets."

Wiezeltier has published 13 volumes of verse and has translated English, French, and Russian poetry into Hebrew. His translations include four of Shakespeare's tragedies, as well as novels by Virginia Woolf, Charles Dickens, E.M. Forster, and Malcolm Lowry. Wiezeltier's poetry can bristle with irony and revel in sarcasm. He often writes in the first person, assuming the at times comic role of a moralist in the midst of a world of chaos and, at other times, the loud and lyrical crusader for personal freedom and an unbridled life amid, for example, the entrenched indoctrination of Masada and the perplexing character of Abraham.

71 A.D.

Son, don't join them: they're sand-blinded slit-throats.[1]
Ignore Ben-Yair's[2] rants and skewed diatribes.
Don't take your family to the lip of a cliff.
Don't use your good robe to hide daggers beneath.

Take your mild wife and comforted children,
find a house in Lod[3] or in Kerem-Yavneh.[4]
Rome stretches from Spain to the Parthian border.
Our Law is Life: don't die by it, but live.[5]

Translated by William Matthews and Moshe Dror

In the year 70 A.D., Rome destroyed the Jewish Temple in Jerusalem and crushed the revolt of the Jews of Judea, which had begun in 66 A.D. The residents of Jerusalem who survived the onslaught were scattered throughout the Roman Empire. The poem was written in 1971.

[1] Referring to the Sicarii (Latin for 'dagger-men'): a violent extremist Jewish political group of the Second Temple Era.

[2] Eleazar Ben-Ya'ir, one of the radical Second Temple Sicarii, later led the (in)famous collective martyrdom/suicide at Masada in the year 73 A.D.

[3] A significant Judean town from the Maccabean Period until the early Christian period, which according to Jewish tradition was the home of the great scholar and teacher Rabbi Akiva.

[4] Yavneh was the town where the leader of the moderate camp, Rabbi Yochanan Ben-Zakkai, established a seminary of Jewish learning that was seen both before and after the destruction of the Second Temple as an alternative to the hawkish nationalist and religious camp of Jerusalem. The Ben-Zakkai Yavneh choice has often been contrasted with the Eliezer ben Yair Masada approach.

[5] Reference to the Judaic dictate that in matters of life or death one is permitted to break all Jewish laws save three: idolatry, murder, incest.

71 לספירה

בְּנִי, אַל תִּסָּפַח אֶל עֲדַת סִיקְרִיקִין בִּתְזָזִית.
אַל תַּטֶּה אֹזֶן לֶלַהֲלוֹהֵי בֶּן־יָאִיר.
אַל תִּקַּח אִשְׁתְּךָ וְטַפְּךָ אֶל רֹאשׁ צוּק בַּמִּדְבָּר.
אַל תַּחְגֹּר פִּגְיוֹנוֹת מְחֻפִּים בַּגְּלִימָה.

טוֹל אִשְׁתְּךָ הָעֲדִינָה וְטַפְּךָ הָרַכִּים,
קַח לְךָ בַּיִת בְּלוֹד אוֹ בְּכֶרֶם יַבְנֶה.
רוֹמִי מוֹשֶׁלֶת מֵאִסְפַּנְיָה עַד גְּבוּל הַפְּרָתִים.
תּוֹרַת חַיִּים, וְחָיִיתָ בָּהּ, וְלֹא בַּמֵּתִים.

To Be Continued

The war is the extension of the policy
and South Lebanon is the extension of Upper Galilee;[1]
therefore it is only natural that a country
will make war in Lebanon.[2]

Youth is the extension of childhood
and South Lebanon is the extension of Upper Galilee;
therefore nothing is more natural than children and boys
shooting each other in Lebanon.

Burial is the extension of the Rabbinate[3]
and South Lebanon is the extension of Upper Galilee;
therefore the military *Hevra Kadisha*[4]
will dig fresh graves in Lebanon.

[1] Southern Lebanon borders on the Northern part of Israel and was a frequent launching pad for Palestinian organizations targeting the upper Galilee region of Israel. This stretch of land in southern Lebanon was sometimes called "Fatahland."

[2] Israeli men and women are drafted at age 18 for compulsory military service of two years for women and three for men.

[3] All burials in Israel are under the supervision of the (Orthodox) rabbinical authorities.

[4] The name of the rabbinical burial society.

המשך יבוא או

הַמִּלְחָמָה הִיא הֶמְשֵׁכָהּ שֶׁל הַמְּדִינִיּוּת,
וּדְרוֹם הַלְּבָנוֹן הֶמְשֵׁכוֹ שֶׁל הַגָּלִיל הָעֶלְיוֹן:
עַל כֵּן אַךְ טִבְעִי שֶׁמְּדִינָה
תַּעֲרֹךְ מִלְחָמָה בַּלְּבָנוֹן.

הַנְּעוּרִים הֵם הֶמְשֵׁכָהּ שֶׁל הַיַּלְדוּת,
וּדְרוֹם הַלְּבָנוֹן הֶמְשֵׁכוֹ שֶׁל הַגָּלִיל הָעֶלְיוֹן:
עַל כֵּן אֵין טִבְעִי מִיְלָדִים וּנְעָרִים
הַיּוֹרִים זֶה בָּזֶה בַּלְּבָנוֹן.

הַקַּבְרָנוּת הִיא הֶמְשֵׁכָהּ שֶׁל הָרַבָּנוּת,
וּדְרוֹם הַלְּבָנוֹן הֶמְשֵׁכוֹ שֶׁל הַגָּלִיל הָעֶלְיוֹן:
עַל כֵּן תִּכְרֶה חֶבְרָה קַדִּישָׁא הַצְּבָאִית
קְבָרִים רַעֲנַנִּים בַּלְּבָנוֹן.

The news media is the extension of prattle
and South Lebanon is the extension of Upper Galilee;
therefore the papers thoughtfully consider
the feats of the war in Lebanon.

Poetry is the opposite of talk
in Lebanon and in the Upper Galilee.
Therefore, what is said is as if it weren't said
and we shall yet go to war in Lebanon.[5]

Translated by Tsipi Keller

[5] This poem was written on April 2, 1978. On June 6, 1982, the First Lebanon War (dubbed by Israel, "Operation Peace for the Galilee") began, in the wake of the attempted assassination of Israel's Ambassador to the UK, Shlomo Argov, by Palestinian gunmen, when Israeli troops entered southern Lebanon in an attempt to quell repeated Fatah attacks on Israel from there.

הָעִתּוֹנוּת הִיא הֶמְשֵׁכָהּ שֶׁל הַפַּטְפְּטָנוּת,
וּדְרוֹם הַלְּבָנוֹן הֶמְשֵׁכוֹ שֶׁל הַגָּלִיל הָעֶלְיוֹן:
עַל כֵּן שׁוֹקְלִים הָעִתּוֹנִים בְּכֹבֶד־רֹאשׁ
אֶת הֶשֵּׂגֵי הַמִּלְחָמָה בַּלְּבָנוֹן.

הַשִּׁירָה הִיא הִפּוּכָהּ שֶׁל הָאֲמִירָה,
בִּדְרוֹם הַלְּבָנוֹן וְגַם בַּגָּלִיל הָעֶלְיוֹן.
עַל כֵּן הַנֶּאֱמָר כְּמוֹ לֹא נֶאֱמַר,
וְעוֹד נֵצֵא לַמִלְחָמָה בַּלְּבָנוֹן.

ISRAEL: VOICES FROM WITHIN

Section 4

A Polyphony
of Voices

The last decades of the 20th century and the first decade of the new millennium were an era of growth and achievement for Israel, coupled with painful discord and conflict. Contemporary Israel is a saga of dramatically diverse voices and stories and, in the words of the late Amos Oz, "a conglomeration of [multiple] blueprints." A state that was populated by approximately 600,000 Jews and 1.15 million non-Jews in 1948 had become a country of over 6 million Jews and 2 million non-Jews by the 21st century and was on the verge of becoming home to the majority of world Jewry. The borderlines of this state on cartographers' maps has constantly changed and is still not agreed upon. The once relatively small *Yishuv* has developed into a much larger heterogeneous state, wrestling with diverse visions of what kind of society this state ought to be.

The dynamics of contemporary Israel have typically been viewed through the lenses of journalists, political scientists, and historians. And yet, as historian Anita Shapira has suggested, Hebrew literature (prose and poetry) is no less of a sensitive and significant seismograph for understanding the mood, ethos, and conscience of contemporary Israeli society.[1] It is in the novels, short stories, and poems of the recent decades that the heartbeat of Israel is heard.

The many poets of today's Israel are characterized by being uncharacteristic.

---

[1] Shapira, *Israel: A History*, 474.

They are multiple voices—some well known and some less well known (with no overpowering Bialik or Amichai)—that tell many tales, sing many psalms, and write many dirges. Indeed, we are witness to entirely new genres of voices: young; feminist; Palestinian; LGBT; Mizrahi, radical left, regular left, center, right, religious, radical right and "just let me be." These voices are as likely to be heard on tablets or cell phones and in intimate venues or outdoor get-togethers as they are to be read in bounded books or discussed in Dizengoff coffee houses. This new age in Israel (like so many ages before!) proposes to be "rebellious" and "anti-institutional" in its way of dealing with gender, economic, and ethnic inequalities, and the excesses of left, right, religious, and secular. At the same time, it preserves the eternal role of poetry in reflecting on issues of life and death, joy and sorrow, and love found and lost and sometimes found again. Stylistically, the new poetry has been influenced by American rap music, spoken word, hip-hop, and new forms and "lingos" of spoken Hebrew. In this section, we will hear the cacophony of multiple voices speaking—sometimes to themselves, sometimes to others, and sometimes to their Maker—but always to us.

Agi Mishol

(1946–)

Agi Mishol was born in Transylvania, Romania, and arrived in Israel as a young child. She has published numerous books of poetry and has won many prizes for her poetry both in Israel and abroad. She is regarded as one of the major and beloved poets of contemporary Israel, and is often referred to as the 'caring mentor of young poets.' She lives on a farm on the coastal plain south of Tel Aviv, near the city of Gadera, where she grows peach and persimmon trees. Mishol's poetry illustrates the local and the universal and manages to touch the hearts and minds of those within and beyond a particular place. Chaim Guri suggested that her poetry possessed a broad poetic spectrum which encompassed "all flora and fauna, near and far, varied and colorful landscapes, love and romance, powerful eroticism, revealing and concealing ... It is poetry filled with rich metaphors and ongoing observation of the human condition."[1]

---

[1] Vered Lee, "Poet Agi Mishol Is Surprised She's Become Hot Stuff," Ha'aretz, May 17, 2012, https://www.haaretz.com/1.5158687

The Interior Plain

Here,
in the interior plain,[1]
I herd in the meadow with my Walkman—
I pick up a stick[2]
split a pomegranate
whistle to the dog

To the list of things that give me goose bumps
I've added this morning Billie Holiday singing
I'm so lonely.

Translated by Tsipi Keller

[1] The *sh'fela* refers to a region in Israel of soft-sloping hills stretching between the Judean Mountains and the Coastal Plain. When presenting nightly weather reports on Israeli television, meteorologists use the term *sh'fela* to refer to temperatures of the area between Tel-Aviv and Jerusalem. The root of the word means "low," which can refer both to a physical state and to an emotional condition.

[2] The prophet Zechariah spoke of two sticks representing two ways of leading the people. One is pleasant and rewarding and the second punishes and rebukes. "And I looked after the sheep to be slaughtered for the sheep traders, and I took me two staffs [sticks]. One I called Pleasantness and the other I called Bruising, and I looked after the sheep." (Zechariah 11:7)

הַשְׁפֵלָה הַפְּנִימִית

כָּאן
בַּשְׁפֵלָה הַפְּנִימִית
אֲנִי רוֹעָה עִם הַוֹּקְמֶן בָּאְזֶן בָּאָחוּ
בּוֹחֶרֶת מַקֵל
מְפַצַּחַת רִמּוֹן
שׁוֹרֶקֶת לַכַּלְבָּה

לִרְשִׁימַת הַדְּבָרִים שֶׁגּוֹרְמִים לִי צַמַרְמֹרֶת
הוֹסַפְתִּי הַבֹּקֶר אֶת בִּילִי הוֹלִידֶיי שָׁרָה
I'm so lonely

November 4, 1995

Something in the shoulders   something outside
weighs down   in the branches
something   some   or the ravens
thing   their voices
in the neck

                                      or something in the world
something *oof*   hard to know
limps in the heart[1]   the pain
de-eep inside
de-eep[2]   something
                                      truly expected[3]

something in the room   sorrow
the things   here
the nearness of objects
or the light   something very
something in the light   *oof*

Translated by Lisa Katz

On November 4, 1995, Israeli Prime Minister Yitzhak Rabin was assassinated by the Jewish extremist Yigal Amir at the end of a mass demonstration in Tel Aviv in support of the peace process.

[1] *Kol od b'leivav p'nima*, "As long as in the heart, within" is part of Israel's national anthem, expresses the perpetual longing of the Jewish people for Zion.

[2] The word means "inside" and the way in which they appear broken into parts echoes the way they are pronounced when sung in the Israeli national anthem, or they might refer to the broken hope.

[3] The word *hara* is associated with being pregnant or being born. The prophet Jeremiah laments having ever been born to witness the misery of the world: "Why from the womb did I come out to see wretchedness and sorrow, and my days end in shame?" (Jeremiah 20:18)

4.11.95

מַשֶּׁהוּ בַּכְּתֵפַיִם
מוֹשֵׁךְ לְמַטָּה
מַשֶּׁהוּ אֵיזֶה דָּבָר
בַּצַּוָּאר

מַשֶּׁהוּ אוּף
שָׁמוּט בַּלֵּבָב
פְּ־נִי־מָה
פְּ־נִי־מָה

מַשֶּׁהוּ בַּחֶדֶר
הַדְּבָרִים
אוֹ שְׁכֵנוּת הַחֲפָצִים
אוֹ הָאוֹר
מַשֶּׁהוּ בָּאוֹר

מַשֶּׁהוּ בַּחוּץ
בָּעֲנָפִים
אוֹ הָעוֹרְבִים
קוֹלָם

אוֹ מַשֶּׁהוּ בָּעוֹלָם
קָשֶׁה לָדַעַת
הַכְּאֵב

מַשֶּׁהוּ הָרֶה מְאֹד
צַעַר
יֵשׁ

מַשֶּׁהוּ אוּף
מְאֹד

Woman Martyr

> The evening goes blind, and you are only twenty.
> *Nathan Alterman, "Late Afternoon in the Market"*

You are only twenty
and your first pregnancy is a bomb.
Under your broad skirt you are pregnant with dynamite
and metal shavings. This is how you walk in the market,
ticking among the people, you, Andaleeb[1] Takatkah.[2]

Someone tinkered with your head
and launched you toward the city;
even though you come from Bethlehem,
the Home of Bread,[3] you chose a bakery.
And there you pulled the trigger out of yourself,
and together with the Sabbath loaves,
sesame and poppy seed,
you flung yourself into the sky.

[1] The name of a female terrorist who exploded a suicide bomb on Friday, April 12, 2002 in the *Mahane Yehuda* Market, Jerusalem's main fruit and vegetable market. Six people were killed and 104 were injured.

[2] The author uses onomatopoeia to connect the name of the terrorist to the "ticking" of the time bomb.

[3] A play on the words *beit lechem*, the name of the city Bethlehem and literally means "house of bread."

שאהידה

"הַעֶרֶב מִתְעַוֵּר/וְאַתְּ רַק בַּת עֶשְׂרִים"

"ערב של שוק," אלתרמן

אַתְּ רַק בַּת עֶשְׂרִים
וְהַהֵרָיוֹן הָרִאשׁוֹן שֶׁלָּךְ הוּא פִּצְצָה.
מִתַּחַת לַשִּׂמְלָה הָרְחָבָה אַתְּ הָרָה חֹמֶר נֶפֶץ,
שְׁבָבִים שֶׁל מַתֶּכֶת, וְכָךְ אַתְּ עוֹבֶרֶת בַּשּׁוּק
מִתַקְתֶּקֶת בֵּין הָאֲנָשִׁים עֲנֻדְלִיב תַּקָאטְקָה.

מִישֶׁהוּ שִׁנָּה לָךְ בָּרֹאשׁ אֶת הַהֶבְרָגָה
וְשִׁגֵּר אוֹתָךְ לָעִיר,
וְאַתְּ שֶׁבָּאת מִבֵּית לֶחֶם, בָּחַרְתְּ לָךְ דַּוְקָא
מַאֲפִיָּה. שָׁם שָׁלַפְתְּ מִתּוֹכֵךְ אֶת הַנִּיצְרָה
וּבְיַחַד עִם חַלּוֹת הַשַּׁבָּת
הַפֶּרֶג וְהַשֻּׁמְשׁוּמִים
הֵעַפְתְּ אֶת עַצְמֵךְ לַשָּׁמַיִם.

Together with Rebecca Fink you flew up
with Yelena Konre'ev from the Caucasus
and Nissim Cohen from Afghanistan
and Suhila Houshy[4] from Iran
and two Chinese you swept along
to death.

Since then, other matters
have obscured your story,
about which I speak all the time
without having anything to say.

Translated by Lisa Katz

[4] The names of victims of the attack reflect the diversity of their origins and nationalities.

בְּיַחַד עִם רִבְקָה פִינְק עָפְתָ,
וַיֵלֵנָה קוֹנְרִיבּ מְחַקְוְקָז,
נִיסִים כֹּהֵן מֵאַפְגָּנִיסְטָן
וְסוּהֵילָה חוֹשִׁי מֵאִירָאן,
וְגַם שְׁנַיִם סִינִים גָּרַפְתְּ אִתָּךְ
אֶל מוֹתֵךְ.

מֵאָז כְּסוּ עִנְיָנִים אַחֵרִים
אֶת הַסִפּוּר שֶׁלָּךְ
שֶׁעָלָיו אֲנִי מְדַבֵּרֶת וּמְדַבֶּרֶת
מִבְּלִי שֶׁיִּהְיֶה לִי מַשֶׁהוּ לְהַגִּיד.

Erez Biton

(1942–)

Erez Biton was born in Oran, Algeria, to Moroccan parents. His family fled Algeria to the town of Lod in Palestine in 1948. At the age of 11, he lost his vision and left hand to a stray grenade. Biton earned a BA in social work from the Hebrew University and an MA in psychology from Bar Ilan University. His poetry is influenced by the richness of the language of North African Jewry: the difficulties faced by his immigrant group in finding its place in contemporary Israeli life, the complex realities of his own life, and his poetic genius. He is the recipient of many of Israel's prestigious awards in poetry.

Yom Kippur at the School for the Blind

Said Mister Shvili the *gabbai*[1] to Mister Cohen:
Here is a day to attend to your soul
attend to the soul of the people
speak in the name of the people
make use of speech
call out and howl
put your soul
and the souls of these people
in the language
these people forged in solitude
forged in fire.
And Mister Cohen, a blind man,
limps on his hip,
all his days like blank pages,
he hobbles with his wife
from day to day.
And we are children
separated from our parents
and their daily hardships,
in a town or in a village,
we replace solitude with prayer,
and Mister Cohen, the faithful emissary,

Yom Kippur, also known as the Day of Atonement, is regarded by many Jews as the holiest day of the year in Judaism. In Israel, there are no radio or television broadcasts, airports are shut down, there is no public transportation, and all shops and businesses are closed. Many Jews observe this holy day with a 25-hour period (approximately) of fasting and intensive prayer, often spending most of the day in synagogue services.

[1] Also known as the *shamash*. A person fulfilling various ritual duties in a synagogue.

יום הכיפורים בבית חינוך עיוורים בירושלים

אָמַר אָדוֹן שְׁויִלי הַגַּבַּאי לְאָדוֹן כֹּהֵן
הִנֵּה זֶה לְךָ יוֹם, עֲשֵׂה בּוֹ נֶפֶשׁ
עֲשֵׂה נֶפֶשׁ לָאֲנָשִׁים
דַּבֵּר בְּשֵׁם הָאֲנָשִׁים
עֲשֵׂה שׁמוֹשׁ בְּכָל הַשָּׂפָה
קְרָא בְּקוֹל וּזְעַק
הַשָּׂפָה בַּשְׁכָּךְ נַפְשֵׁן תֵּן
שָׁשׁ נַפְשֵׁן תֵּן
וְהָאֲנָשִׁים הָאֵלֶּה
יְצוּקִים מִבְּדִידוּת צְרוּפָה
יְצוּקִים מְשֻׁרְפַָה.
וְאָדוֹן כֹּהֵן אִישׁ עֵרֶב,
צוֹלֵעַ עַל יְרֵכוֹ,
שֶׁכָּל יָמָיו כְּמוֹ דַּפִּים רֵיקִים,
מִדַּדֶּה עִם שְׁאוֹ
לְהַעֲבִיר יוֹם וְעוֹד יוֹם.
וַאֲנַחְנוּ יְלָדִים
עֲזוּבִים מֵהוֹרֵינוּ
הַנִּתוּנִים בְּמִצוּקָתָם,
אֶחָד בְּעִיר וְאֶחָד בִּכְפָר
וַאֲנַחְנוּ מְמִירים
בְּדִידוּת בְּתִפְלָה,
וְאָדוֹן כֹּהֵן, הַמְתַקֵּךְ הַנֶּאֱמָן

drains sorrows and paves the way
between us and veiled hopes,
his prayer transforming the pain
of solitude into bashful beauty.
And we know that like a shimmering butterfly
drawn to the light
Mister Cohen too will give all that he has,
his entire being,[2]
and we know that
at the end of the day
with the blowing of the shofar
Mister Cohen yet again
will limp on his hip
toward his home
at the edge of the neighborhood
where together with his blind spouse
he will live day to day
through days of blank pages
until Yom Kippur comes around again.

Translated by Tsipi Keller

[2] The Hebrew uses words from the *Sh'ma* prayer: "And you shall love the LORD your God with all your heart and with all your being and with all your might." (Deuteronomy 6:5)

מְנַקֵּז צַעַר, מְפַלֵּס דֶּרֶךְ
בֵּינֵינוּ לְבֵין תִּקְוָה נַעֲלָמָה.
בְּתִפְלָתוֹ הָיָה הוֹפֵךְ
אֶת צַעַר הַבְּדִידוּת לְיֹפִי נִכְלָם.
וַאֲנַחְנוּ יוֹדְעִים, שֶׁכְּמוֹ פַּרְפָּר כָּסוּף,
הַמֵּיטִיב לָצֵאת אֶל הָאוֹר,
גַּם אָדוֹן כֹּהֵן יִתֵּן אֶת כָּל כֻּלּוֹ
וְאֶת כָּל מְאוֹדוֹ
וַאֲנַחְנוּ יוֹדְעִים
כִּי עִם תְּקִיעַת הַשּׁוֹפָר
בְּסוֹף הַיּוֹם
שׁוּב יְדַדֶּה אָדוֹן כֹּהֵן
צוֹלֵעַ עַל יְרֵכוֹ
אֶל בֵּיתוֹ בִּקְצֵה הָרֹבַע
שָׁם
יַחַד עִם אִשְׁתּוֹ הָעֵרֶת
יַעֲבִיר עוֹד יוֹם וְעוֹד יוֹם
בְּיָמִים שֶׁהֵם דַּפִּים רֵיקִים
עַד לְיוֹם הַכִּפּוּרִים הַבָּא.

A Purchase on Dizengov

I purchased a store on Dizengov
to strike roots
to purchase roots
to find me a perch in Roval
but
the people in Roval[1]
I ask myself
who are these people in Roval
what's so special about these people in Roval
what make them tick these people in Roval
I don't address the people in Roval
and when the people in Roval address me
I pull out the language,[2]
clean words,
a most up-to-date Hebrew,

Dizengoff Street, named after Tel Aviv's first mayor, Meir Dizengoff (1861–1936), is a major thoroughfare in Tel Aviv. In the street's heyday, it was described as the "Champs-Élysées of Tel Aviv." Biton consciously misspells the name of the street in Hebrew to hint at prevalent Ashkenazi prejudices regarding the literacy and language of immigrants from North Africa.

[1] Roval, a European-style café, opened in 1948 on Dizengoff Street and became renowned for its pastries. It was a popular meeting place for the political, bohemian, and bourgeois society of Tel Aviv until it closed in 1980.

[2] The word used by Biton is *sholef* (i.e., I "draw" out the language, I make it sound classy and Western).

שיר קנייה בדיזנגוב

קָנִיתִי חֲנוּת בְּדִיזְנְגּוֹב

כְּדֵי לְהַכּוֹת שֹׁרֶשׁ

כְּדֵי לִקְנוֹת שֹׁרֶשׁ

כְּדֵי לִמְצֹא מָקוֹם בְּרֹוַּל

אֲבָל

הָאֲנָשִׁים בְּרֹוַּל

אֲנִי שׁוֹאֵל אֶת עַצְמִי

מִי הֵם הָאֲנָשִׁים בְּרֹוַּל,

מַה יֵּשׁ בָּאֲנָשִׁים בְּרֹוַּל,

מַה הוֹלֵךְ בָּאֲנָשִׁים בְּרֹוַּל,

אֲנִי לֹא פּוֹנֶה לָאֲנָשִׁים בְּרֹוַּל

כְּשֶׁהָאֲנָשִׁים בְּרֹוַּל פּוֹנִים אֵלַי

אֲנִי שׁוֹלֵף אֶת הַשָּׂפָה

מִלִּים נְקִיּוֹת,

Yes, sir,
Welcome, sir,[3]
and here the buildings loom over me
they tower over me
and here the open entryways
are inaccessible to me
here.
At nightfall
in the store on Dizengov
I pack my things
to go back to the outskirts
to the other Hebrew.

Translated by Tsipi Keller

[3] This greeting was associated with a Hebrew style (similar to *vous* or *sie*) which was frequently used by German-speaking immigrants, often called *yekkes*. It suggests a formalistic and somewhat condescending linguistic affectation.

כֵּן אֲדוֹנִי,

בְּבַקָּשָׁה אֲדוֹנִי,

עִבְרִית מְעֻדְכֶּנֶת מְאוֹד,

וְהַבָּתִּים הָעוֹמְדִים כָּאן עָלַי

גְּבוֹהִים כָּאן עָלַי,

וְהַפְּתָחִים הַפְּתוּחִים כָּאן

בִּלְתֵּי חֲדִירִים לִי כָּאן

בְּשָׁעָה אֲפֵלוּלִית

בַּחֲנוּת בְּדִיזְנְגּוֹב

אֲנִי אוֹרֵז חֲפָצִים

לַחֲזֹר לַפַּרְבָּרִים

לְעִבְרִית הָאַחֶרֶת.

Tuvia Rubner

(1924–2019)

Tuvia Rubner immigrated to Palestine in 1941 from Bratislava, Czechoslovakia, leaving behind the other members of his family, who were murdered by the Nazis. He was a poet and translator who lived in Kibbutz Merhavia (once the kibbutz of Golda Meir). He was a longstanding, wise, and reflective commentator on pre-and post-State Israel for many decades. Rubner was the recipient of every major literary prize in Israel. He published his 17th book of poetry, *Od Lo Od,* a few months prior to his death at the age of 95.

*

This is not what we wanted, no, no, not this.
Without them, who are we and for what?
We didn't want this, no, not this, we didn't think it would be like this:
how the land just devours and devours.[1]

Translated by Rachel Tzvia Back

[1] The language here echoes the biblical story of a rebellious figure named Korach. "And it happened, just as he finished speaking all these words, the ground that was under them split apart, and the earth opened its mouth and swallowed them and their households and every human being that was Korach's, and all the possessions. And they went down, they and all that was theirs, alive to Sheol, and the earth covered over them, and they perished from the midst of the assembly." (Numbers 16:31–33)

זֹאת לֹא רָצִינוּ, לֹא, זֹאת לֹא רָצִינוּ.
בִּלְעֲדֵיהֶם מָה אָנוּ וּלְשֵׁם מָה?
לֹא כָּךְ חָשַׁבְנוּ, לֹא רָצִינוּ, לֹא, זֹאת לֹא רָצִינוּ
שֶׁכָּךְ תִּבְלַע הָאֲדָמָה.

Salman Masalha
(1953–)

Salman Masalha was born to a Druze family in the town of al-Maghar, an Arab town in the Galilee. In 1972 he moved to Jerusalem, earning a PhD from the Hebrew University in classical Arabic literature. He has authored poetry collections in both Arabic and Hebrew, in addition to translating poetry in both directions. Masalha is a frequent contributor to the editorial pages of *Ha'aretz* and *Al-Hayat*. His book, *In Place,* won the Prime Minister's Award in 2008.

One from Here

A poem for the late hours of the night

It changes so fast,
the world. And for me it's
now absurd. Things have got
to the point that I've stopped
thinking about fall. Because, after all, from here,
there's nowhere to go.
And anyway, even in the park
the trees are uprooted[1] and gone.

And at times like these, it's dangerous
to go out in the streets in this country.
The road is so wet.
Blood flows in the main artery.
I count them:
One from here, one from there.
I count them
like sheep, until
I fall asleep.

Translated by Vivian Eden

[1] While uprooting trees in Israel without a permit is illegal and considered a criminal offense, there have been numerous instances of such infractions.

אחד מכאן

שיר לשעת לילה מאוחרת

כָּל כָּךְ מַהֵר הִשְׁתַּנָּה
הָעוֹלָם. וְאֶצְלִי, זֶה כְּבָר
מֻגְזָם. הַדְּבָרִים הִגִּיעוּ
עַד כְּדֵי כָּךְ, שֶׁהִפְסַקְתִּי
לַחְשֹׁב עַל שַׁלֶּכֶת. כִּי
הֲרֵי מִכָּאן, אֵין לְאָן
לָלֶכֶת. וּמִמֵּילָא, גַּם
בַּגַּן, הָעֵצִים נֶעֶקְרוּ
וְאֵינָם.

וּבְיָמִים כָּאֵלֶּה, מִסְכָּן
לָצֵאת בָּאָרֶץ לָרְחוֹב.
הַכְּבִישׁ כָּל כָּךְ רָטֹב.
דָּם זוֹרֵם בָּעוֹרֵק הָרָאשִׁי.
אֲנִי סוֹפֵר אוֹתָם:
אֶחָד מִכָּאן, אֶחָד מִשָּׁם.
אֲנִי סוֹפֵר אוֹתָם,
כְּמוֹ כְּבָשִׂים, עַד
שֶׁאֲנִי נִרְדָּם.

Eliaz Cohen

(1972–)

Eliaz Cohen was born in Petach Tikvah into a religious-Zionist family and at age seven moved with his family to the West Bank settlement of Elkana. As a child, he studied Arabic and befriended Arab children in nearby villages. These experiences and relationships remained central to him, leading him during his military service to create and train his fellow soldiers in "humane check point conduct," conveying the importance of the people-to-people interaction at the check point. Following the army, Eliaz returned to the Yeshiva and later received a degree in social work. He served as editor of *Mashiv Haruach*, a journal that features the writings of observant Israelis addressing religious and moral issues related to post-1967 Israel. His poetry suggests a classic motif found in Jewish literature throughout the ages of talking to and even "arguing" with God. In 2006, he received the Prime Minister's Prize in poetry.

Hear, O Lord

(prayer for days of awe)

Hear, O Lord, Israel, your people, Israel is one[1]

And you shall love Israel your people[2]
With all your heart
And with all your soul
And with all your might
And these sons who are being killed for you daily shall be
upon your heart
And you shall teach them diligently in your heavens
And you shall talk of them:
When you sit in your house
And when you walk by the way
And when you lie down and when you rise
And you shall bind them as a sign upon
your hand (phosphorescent blue numbers)[3] and they shall be as frontlets
between your eyes (like the sniper's shot)[4]
And you shall write them (in blood) on the doorposts of your house[5]
And on your gates

Translated by Larry Barak

Cohen's poem was written in 2004 during the Palestinian uprising known as the Second Intifada.

[1] This line is based on the Shema prayer: "Hear O Israel, The LORD Our God the LORD is One" but it is Israel who is commanding God rather than the other way around.

[2] New words not in the original Shema prayer are added.

[3] Suggests the number tattooed on the arms of concentration camp prisoners.

[4] Reference to a sharpshooter's gun aiming at a specific target.

[5] The poem adds the words "in blood" to the original Shema prayer suggesting the tenth plague in Egypt when Israelites placed blood on their doorposts protecting them from the plague (Exodus 12:7).

שְׁמַע אֲדֹ־נָי

(ייחוד לימים נוראים)

שְׁמַע אֲדֹ־נָי, יִשְׂרָאֵל עַמֶּךְ יִשְׂרָאֵל אֶחָד

וְאָהַבְתָּ אֶת יִשְׂרָאֵל עַמֶּךְ

בְּכָל לְבָבְךְ

וּבְכָל נַפְשְׁךְ

וּבְכָל מְאֹדֶךְ

וְהָיוּ הַבָּנִים הָאֵלֶּה אֲשֶׁר נֶהֱרָגִים עָלֶיךְ כָּל הַיֹּום

עַל לְבָבֶךְ

וְשִׁנַּנְתָּם בִּרְקִיעֶיךְ

וְדִבַּרְתָּ בָּם:

בְּשִׁבְתְּךְ בְּבֵיתֶךְ

וּבְלֶכְתְּךְ בַּדֶּרֶךְ

וּבְשָׁכְבְּךְ וּבְקוּמֶךְ

וּקְשַׁרְתָּם לְאֹות עַל

יָדֶךְ (סְפָרוֹת כְּחֻלּוֹת זַרְחָנִיּוֹת) וְהָיוּ לטטפות בֵּין

עֵינֶיךְ (כְּמוֹ פְּגִיעַת הַצַּלָּפִים)

וּכְתַבְתָּם (בְּדָם) עַל־מְזֻזוֹת בֵּיתֶךְ

וּבִשְׁעָרֶיךְ

With Me From Lebanon

(A Memorial Poem)[1]

Every one has his own Lebanon
a handsome dead soldier carried on my shoulders
I brought
with me from Lebanon.
His names mumble to me I do not want to remember
       his face

every one has his own Lebanon
a scratch on his soul
I remember only the rocks, the ascent
              Br ea th
ing hard falling on the thorns and he upon me and he
with me from Lebanon

Yoav.
At morning, a light tapping waking his soldiers.
Sharpening the end of a pencil, on a blank sheet of paper a world is
       recorded now:
       tensed faces, a ram caught in the green tree.
Dust and the smell of blood rising from an ambush.
       He died handsome, Yoav.

[1] In this poem, the poet reflects on his military service in occupied Southern Lebanon.

אִתִּי מִלְּבָנוֹן

(פואמת זיכרון)

כָּל אֶחָד יֵשׁ לוֹ אֶת הַלְּבָנוֹן שֶׁלּוֹ
חַיָּל יָפֶה הָרוּג נִשָּׂא עַל הַכְּתֵפַיִם
הֵבֵאתִי
אִתִּי מִלְּבָנוֹן.
שְׁמוֹתָיו מְמַלְמְלִים אֵלַי לֹא אֶרְצֶה לִזְכֹּר
פָּנָיו

כָּל אֶחָד יֵשׁ לוֹ אֶת הַלְּבָנוֹן שֶׁלּוֹ
שֹׂרֶט בַּנֶּפֶשׁ
אֲנִי זוֹכֵר רַק אֶת הַסְּלָעִים, הָעֲלָיָה
מֵ תְ
נַ שֵׁף נוֹפֵל עַל הַקּוֹצִים וְהוּא עָלַי וְהוּא
אִתִּי מִלְּבָנוֹן

יוֹאָב.
בַּבְּקָרִים, טְפִיחוֹת קַלּוֹת מֵעִיר אֶת חַיָּלָיו.
מַשְׁחִיז קָצֶה שֶׁל עִפָּרוֹן, עַל דַּף חָלָק נִרְשָׁם עוֹלָם עַכְשָׁו:
פָּנִים שֶׁנִּדְרְכוּ, אַיִל נֶאֱחָז בַּעֵץ הַמַּלְבְּלָב.
אָבָק וְרֵיחַ דָּם עוֹלִים מִמַּאֲרָב.
הוּא מֵת יָפֶה, יוֹאָב.

A spot on his forehead, like an Indian girl promised to a man they
	did not harm
the freckles the body continued to attack like a panther
and Lebanon with me is not sufficient to burn

Every one has his own Lebanon
	an embryo grows stabs
		so you'll remember!

Open Lebanon your doors[2] and all my winged
visionary soldiers will come
	and they will be planted in you like cedars.
Like Yoav like
	Nadav.

His look is like that of Lebanon and who has betrothed a wife and has not taken her
with him in a tongue of flame wants to shout with me
from Lebanon my bride with me
from Lebanon come
clothed with the slain, those pierced by the sword,
the garments of living widowhood

[2] "Open, O Lebanon, your doors, that fire consume your cedars." (Zechariah 11:1)

נְקֻדָּה בַּמֵּצַח, כְּמוֹ נַעֲרָה הֲדִית מִיעֶדֶת לְאִישׁ לֹא פָּגְעוּ
בַּנְּמָשִׁים הַגּוּף עוֹד הַמְשִׁיךְ לְהִסְתָּעֵר כְּמוֹ פֻּנְתֵּר
וּלְבָנוֹן אִתִּי אֵין דַּי בַּעֵר

כָּל אֶחָד יֵשׁ לוֹ אֶת הַלְּבָנוֹן שֶׁלּוֹ
עָבָר גַּדֵל דּוֹקֵר
שֶׁתִּזָּכֵר!

פְּתַח לְבָנוֹן דְּלָתֶיךָ וְיָבוֹאוּ כָּל חַיָּלַי
הַמְכַנְּפִים הַמְהַזִּים
וְיִנָּטְעוּ בְּךָ כָּאֲרָזִים.
כְּמוֹ יוֹאָב כְּמוֹ
נָדָב.

מַרְאֵהוּ כַּלְּבָנוֹן וּמִי שֶׁאֵרֵשׂ אִשָּׁה וְלֹא לְקָחָהּ עִמּוֹ בְּלַהַב
אֵשׁ רוֹצֶה לִצְעֹק אִתִּי
מִלְּבָנוֹן כַּלָּה אִתִּי
מִלְּבָנוֹן תָּבוֹאִי
תִּלְבְּשִׁי לְבוּשׁ הֲרוּגִים מְטֹעֲנֵי חֶרֶב
לְבוּשׁ אַלְמְנוּת חַיָּת

why has your face darkened Lebanon the dawn does not rise caught
in the fog lowering a curtain on memory, a heretic flash.
Yossi.
Sitting in a patrol jeep long flexible legs gathered to
      the deer-like body of a good Ashdod boy.
Doing a radio check with God.[3]
      God come in, over.
After *havdalah*[4] he makes me coffee. Infantry instant.
      The difference an instant makes?!
      Yossi.

All night the fire burned consuming the cedars of Lebanon
      identifying Danoch by the white teeth of his smile
Lebanon became gutted withered charred
      when a seed was buried in his father in the embrace of souls
and may the Lord guard them
      when flames flared up in Moshe and Eran[5]

[3] The poet compares frequent tests ("radio checks" of the strength and clarity of military voice communication systems) with his ongoing "checks" with his God.

[4] Havdalah is a prayer recited Saturday evening to distinguish between the holiness of the Sabbath and the normalcy of the week. For the poet, it symbolizes the paradox in the holy and the profane nature of his life as a soldier protecting his country while at the same time remaining committed to moral and spiritual teachings.

[5] Names of friends and comrades in the unit.

לָמָה קָדְרוּ פָּנֶיךָ לְבָנוֹן הַשַּׁחַר לֹא עוֹלֶה נֶאֱחָז
בַּעֲרָפֶל מוֹרִיד וִילוֹן עַל זִכָּרוֹן, הֶבְזֵק אֶפִּיקוֹרְסִי.
יוֹסִי.
בְּגִ'יפּ סִי יוּר יוֹשֵׁב רַגְלַיִם אֲרֻכּוֹת גְּמִישׁוֹת כְּנוּסוֹת אֶל
גּוּף צְבָיִי שֶׁל יֶלֶד טוֹב אַשְׁדּוֹד.
עוֹשֶׂה בְּדִיקַת קֶשֶׁר עִם אֱלֹהִים.
אֱלֹהִים שׁוֹמֵעַ, עָבֵר.
אַחֲרֵי הַהַבְדָּלָה מֵכִין לִי נֵס. נֵס רוֹבָאִית.
אֵיזֶה נֵס! אֵילוּ נִסִּים?
יוֹסִי.

כָּל הַלַּיְלָה בָּעֲרָה הָאֵשׁ וַתֹּאכַל אֶת אַרְזֵי הַלְּבָנוֹן
אֶת דָּנוּךְ זָהֲתָה לְפִי הַשָּׁנִים הַלְּבָנוֹת שֶׁבַּחְיַיךָ
הֶחְפִּיר לְבָנוֹן קָמַל הָפַךְ חָרוּךְ
כְּשֶׁזֶּרַע נִטְמַן בְּאָבִיו בְּחִבּוּק הַנְּפָשׁוֹת וְאֵל יִשְׁמְרָן
עֵת לָקְחוּ שַׁלְהָבוֹת בְּמֹשֶׁה וְעֶרָן

every one has his own Lebanon
        a burning heart that is not consumed
once I returned there:
to Lebanon in a tank like a young wild ox
        and I found.
In the birch tree a ram's horn was held. The ram fled[6]
        (like the leg of Itamar which remained in the thicket)
she is opposite me in the living room, above the books
        she guards against my lowering of a curtain.
Or on another occasion, opposite the Syrian Hermon
        I am *tefillin* in a Greek temple a military post penetrating
the heavens

where are you, mother
go up to Lebanon and shout

And those who are going will not let go
        I go with them
                against my will

every one has his own Lebanon
        a handsome dead soldier carried on my shoulders
and all his girls whisper his names and he is upon me and he
        is with me from Lebanon

4th of Iyar, 5760[7]

Translated by Larry Barak

[6] Reference to the proposed sacrifice of Isaac by his father Abraham (Genesis 22:1–19), which became a powerful leitmotif in contemporary Israeli art, poetry, and film.

[7] The 4th of Iyar is Yom Hazikaron, Israel's Memorial Day for Fallen Soldiers and Victims of Terror. During the Hebrew year 5760 (which is equivalent to the Gregorian year 1999-2000), Yom Hazikaron fell on May 10th, two weeks before the unilateral Israeli withdrawal from Lebanon on May 24th, 2000.

כָּל אֶחָד יֵשׁ לוֹ אֶת הַלְּבָנוֹן שֶׁלוֹ
לֵב בּוֹעֵר וְאֵינֶנּוּ אֻכָּל
פַּעַם אַחַת חָזַרְתִּי לְשָׁם:
לִלְבָנוֹן בְּשִׁרְיוֹן כְּמוֹ בֶּן רְאֵמִים
וּמְצָאתִי.
בַּלְּבָנָה נֶאֱחָזָה קֶרֶן שֶׁל אַיִל. הָאַיִל בָּרַח
(כְּמוֹ הָרֶגֶל שֶׁל אִיתָמָר שֶׁנּוֹתְרָה בַּסְּבַךְ)
הִיא מוּלִי בַּסָּלוֹן, מֵעַל הַסְּפָרִים
שׁוֹמֶרֶת שֶׁלֹּא אוֹרִיד מָסָךְ.
אוֹ פַּעַם אַחֵר, מוּל חֶרְמוֹן הַסּוּרִי
אֲנִי תְּפִלִּין בְּמִקְדָּשׁ יְוָנִי מְצַב חוֹדֵר
אֶת הַשָּׁמַיִם

אֵיפֹה אַתְּ, אִמָּא
עֲלִי הַלְּבָנוֹן וְצַעֲקִי

וְהַהוֹלְכִים אֵינָם מְנִיחִים
אֲנִי הוֹלֵךְ אוֹתָם
בְּעַל־כָּרְחִי

כָּל אֶחָד יֵשׁ לוֹ אֶת הַלְּבָנוֹן שֶׁלוֹ
חַיָל יָפֶה הָרוּג נִשָּׂא עַל הַכְּתֵפַיִם
וְכָל נַעֲרוֹתָיו מְלַחֲשׁוֹת בְּאֹזֶן אֶת שְׁמוֹתָיו וְהוּא עָלַי וְהוּא
אִתִּי מִלְּבָנוֹן

ד באייר התש"ס

Ronny Someck

(1951–)

Ronny Someck was born in Baghdad and immigrated to Israel as a child. He studied Hebrew literature and philosophy at Tel Aviv University, where he has also taught literature. In addition to writing poetry, he is a recognized painter. His poetry has been translated into 41 languages, and he is the recipient of numerous literary awards in Israel and abroad. His poetry combines an array of linguistic and cultural forms: street Hebrew, Palestinian Arabic, and Iraqi Jewish language and culture, alongside American pop culture including Johnny Weissmuller (the first Tarzan), Alfred Hitchcock, Elvis Presley, and Billie Holiday. His writings are a bricolage of the streets and neighborhoods of contemporary Tel Aviv and the multiplicity of sounds, sights, and scenery that comprise Israel today.

Poverty Line

As if one could draw a line and say: under it
is poverty. Here's the bread wearing cheap makeup
turning black
and here are the olives on a small plate
on the tablecloth.
In the air pigeons fly in salute[1]
to the clanging bell from the kerosene vendor's red cart
and there is the squishing sound of rubber boots landing in mud.
I was a child, in a house called a shack, in a neighborhood
called transit camp for immigrants. The only line
I saw was the horizon, and under it everything seemed
poverty.

Translated by Moshe Dor and Barbara Goldberg

The phrase *kav ha'oni* literally translates as "the poverty line" and it refers to the minimum level of household income beneath which one is formally considered poor. This figure, based on total earnings and total number of dependents in the household, is used to decide who is entitled to government subsidies for food, shelter, and utilities.

[1] On Independence Day, the Israeli Air Force often conducts a salute in the skies of the country, in which dozens of aircraft take part.

קַו הָעֹנִי

כְּאִלּוּ אֶפְשָׁר לִמְתֹחַ קַו וְלוֹמַר: מִתַּחְתָּיו הָעֹנִי.
הִנֵּה הַלֶּחֶם שֶׁבְּצִבְעֵי אֵפוֹר זוֹלִים
נִהְיָה שָׁחֹר
וְהַזֵּיתִים בְּצַלַּחַת קְטַנָּה
עַל מַפַּת הַשֻּׁלְחָן.
בָּאֲוִיר, עֲפוּ יוֹנִים בְּמֶטַס הַצְּדָעָה
לִצְלִילֵי הַפַּעֲמוֹן שֶׁבְּיַד מוֹכֵר הַנֵּפְט בָּעֲגָלָה הָאֲדֻמָּה,
וְהָיָה גַּם קוֹל הַנְחִיתָה שֶׁל מַגְּפֵי הַגּוּמִי בַּאֲדָמָה הַבִּצִּית.
הָיִיתִי יֶלֶד, בַּבַּיִת שֶׁקָּרְאוּ לוֹ צְרִיף,
בַּשְּׁכוּנָה שֶׁאָמְרוּ עָלֶיהָ מַעְבָּרָה.
הַקַּו הַיָּחִיד שֶׁרָאִיתִי הָיָה קַו הָאֹפֶק וּמִתַּחְתָּיו הַכֹּל נִרְאָה
עֹנִי.

Punctures of History in the Valley of Yehoshafat

The British called the Valley of Yehoshafat — *Josafat*,[1]
the Arabs shortened it to *Wadi Joz*
and the Jews named it in Hebrew *Nahal Egoz*.[2]
Because of its many names the earth's womb took in its waters
as a woman's body takes in the scents
of her lovers
but now she slumbers in the dark heart
of a car trunk, like a spare tire
waiting for the next historical puncture
to call forth her existence.

Translated by Moshe Dor and Barbara Goldberg

The title of the poem uses the word *puncher*, which is local slang for a flat tire, taken from the British-English word "puncture."

[1] The Valley of *Yehoshafat*, called *Wadi Joz* in Arabic, is replete with car repair shops, which, over the years, have been frequented by Israeli and Palestinian clientele. It is part of the Kidron Valley located between the Old City of Jerusalem and the Mount of Olives, and is cited in the Book of Joel (4:12) as the place where all nations will be judged and where God will chastise the enemies of Israel.

[2] When the State of Israel was founded, it often Hebraized the Arabic names of places, and *Wadi Joz* was (mistakenly) translated as *Nahal Egoz*.

הַפַּנְצֶ'רִים שֶׁל הַהִיסְטוֹרְיָה בְּעֵמֶק יְהוֹשָׁפָט

הָאַנְגְּלִים קָרְאוּ לְעֵמֶק יְהוֹשָׁפָט –גֹ'וֹזֶפָט

הָעֲרָבִים קִצְרוּ לְוָאדִי גֹ'וז

וְהַיְּהוּדִים עִבְרְתוּ לְנַחַל אֱגוֹז.

מֵרֹב שֵׁמוֹת נִסְפְּגוּ הַמַּיִם בְּבֶטֶן הָאֲדָמָה

כְּמוֹ הָיוּ מִינֵי בְּשָׂמִים שֶׁהִתִּיזוּ מְאַהֲבִים רַבִּים

עַל גּוּף אִשָּׁה

וּבֵינְתַיִם, הִיא נָחָה כְּגַלְגַּל רֶזֶרְבִי

בְּלֵב תָּא הַמִּטְעָן,

מְחַכָּה לַפַּנְצֶ'ר הַהִיסְטוֹרִי הַבָּא

שֶׁיַּזְכִּיר אֶת קִיּוּמָהּ.

Mahmoud Darwish

(1941–2008)

Mahmoud Darwish was born on March 13, 1941 in the village of al-Birwa in the Western Galilee. In June 1948, his family fled to Lebanon, returning a year later to the Acre (Akko) area. Darwish published his first book of poetry at the age of 19 in Haifa. Darwish left Israel in 1970 to study in the Soviet Union, subsequently moving to Egypt and Lebanon, where he joined the PLO (Palestine Liberation Organization). Darwish published more than 30 volumes of poetry and eight books of prose, and he was the editor of several periodicals, including some literary magazines in Israel. Darwish indicated that his poetry was influenced by Iraqi poets Abd al-Wahhab Al-Bayati and Badr Shakir al-Sayyab, French poet Arthur Rimbaud, and 20th century American poet Allen Ginsberg. Darwish is widely regarded as the Palestinian national poet.

This Is Forgetfulness

This is forgetfulness around you: billboards
awakening the past, urging remembrance. Reigning in
the speeding time at traffic lights,
and closing up the squares /

A marble statue is forgetfulness. A statue
staring at you: Stand up as I do to look like me.
And place roses on my feet /

A hackneyed song is forgetfulness. A song
chasing the housewife in celebration of the happy
occasion, in the bed and in the VCR room,
and in her vacant salon, and in her kitchen /

And a monument is forgetfulness. Monuments
on the roads shaped like bronze trees
adorned with eulogies and eagles /

And a museum empty of tomorrow, cold,
narrating the seasons already chosen from the start.
This is forgetfulness: that you remember the past
and not remember tomorrow in the story.

Translated by Dr. Foady Joudah

זוהי השכחה

זוֹהִי הַשִּׁכְחָה סְבִיבְךָ: כְּרָזוֹת
מְעוֹרְרוֹת אֶת הֶעָבָר, מְדַרְבְּנוֹת לְהִזָּכֵר. מְרַסְּנוֹת
אֶת הַזְּמַן הַמָּהִיר עַל תַּמְרוּרֵי הַדְּרָכִים,
וְחוֹסְמוֹת אֶת הַכִּכָּרוֹת /

הַשִּׁכְחָה הִיא פֶּסֶל שַׁיִשׁ. פֶּסֶל
שֶׁמִּתְבּוֹנֵן בְּךָ: עָמַד כָּמוֹנִי וְתִדְמֶה לִי.
וְהִנַּח שׁוֹשַׁנִּים לְרַגְלַי /

הַשִּׁכְחָה הִיא פִּזְמוֹן חוֹזֵר. פִּזְמוֹן
שֶׁרוֹדֵף אַחַר עֲקֶרֶת הַבַּיִת הַשְּׂמֵחָה עַל רֶגַע
מְאֻשָּׁר, בַּמִּטָּה, בַּחֲדַר הַטֵּלֵוִיזְיָה,
בַּחֲדַר הָאוֹרְחִים הָרֵיק, וּבְמִטְבָּחָהּ /

הַשִּׁכְחָה הִיא אַנְדַּרְטָאוֹת. אַנְדַּרְטָאוֹת עַל
הַדְּרָכִים לוּבְשׁוֹת עֲצֵי נְחֹשֶׁת
עֲטוּרִים דִּבְרֵי שֶׁבַח וּקְלָלוֹת /

וּמוּזֵיאוֹן רֵיק מֵהַמָּחָר, קַר,
הַמְסַפֵּר פְּרָקִים שֶׁנִּבְחֲרוּ מֵהַהַתְחָלָה
זוֹהִי הַשִּׁכְחָה: שֶׁתִּזְכֹּר אֶת הֶעָבָר
וְלֹא תִזְכֹּר אֶת הַמָּחָר בַּסִּפּוּר.

Don't Write History as Poetry

Don't write history as poetry, because the weapon is
the historian. And the historian doesn't get fever
chills when he names his victims, and doesn't listen
to the guitar's rendition. And history is the dailiness
of weapons prescribed upon our bodies. "The
intelligent genius is the mighty one." And history
has no compassion that we can long for our
beginning, and no intention that we can know what's ahead
and what's behind... and it has no rest stops
by the railroad tracks for us to bury the dead, for us to look
toward what time has done to us over there, and what
we've done to time. As if we were of it and outside it.
History is not logical or intuitive that we can break
what is left of our myth about happy times,
nor is it a myth that we can accept our dwelling at the doors
of judgement day. It is in us and outside us... and a mad
repetition, from the catapult to the nuclear thunder.
Aimlessly we make it and it makes us... Perhaps
history wasn't born as we desired, because
the Human Being never existed?
Philosophers and artists passed through there...

אל תכתוב את ההיסטוריה בשיר

אַל תִּכְתֹּב אֶת הַהִיסְטוֹרְיָה בְּשִׁיר, שֶׁהֲרֵי הַנֶּשֶׁק הוּא
הַהִיסְטוֹרְיוֹן. וְהַהִיסְטוֹרְיוֹן אֵינוּ נִתְקָף בְּצַמַּרְמֹרֶת חֹם
כַּאֲשֶׁר הוּא נוֹקֵב בִּשְׁמוֹת קָרְבְּנוֹתָיו
וְאֵינוּ מַטֶּה אֹזֶן לְסִפּוּר הַגִּיטָרָה.
וְהַהִיסְטוֹרְיָה הִיא יוֹמְנֵי
נֶשֶׁק שֶׁנִּרְשְׁמוּ עַל גּוּפוֹתֵינוּ.
"הֶפְקֵחַ הַגָּאוֹן הוּא הֶחָזָק". וְלַהִיסְטוֹרְיָה
אֵין רֶגֶשׁ שֶׁנָּחוּשׁ גַּעְגּוּעִים
לְרֵאשִׁיתֵנוּ, וְלֹא כִּוּוּן שֶׁנֵּדַע מַה קָּדִימָה
וּמַה אָחוֹרָה... וּבְמְסִילּוֹת הַבַּרְזֶל
אֵין חֶנְיוֹנִים שֶׁנִּקְבֹּר בָּהֶם אֶת הַמֵּתִים, וְנַבִּיט
לְעֵבֶר מַה שֶׁהַזְּמַן עוֹלֵל לָנוּ,
וּמַה שֶׁאָנוּ עוֹלַלְנוּ לַזְּמַן. כְּאִלּוּ אָנוּ חֵלֶק מִמֶּנָּה וְגַם מְחוּצָה לָהּ.
אֵין הִיא הֶגְיוֹנִית אוֹ מוּבֶנֶת מֵאֵלֶיהָ, שֶׁנְּנַפֵּץ
אֶת מַה שֶׁנּוֹתַר מֵאַגָּדָתֵנוּ עַל אוֹדוֹת הַזְּמַן הַמְאָשָּׁר,
וְאֵין הִיא אֱמוּנַת הֶבֶל, שֶׁנִּרְצֶה בְּהִסְתּוֹפְפוּת בְּשַׁעֲרֵי
הַתְּקוּמָה. הִיא בְּתוֹכֵנוּ וּמְחוּצָה לָנוּ... וַחֲזָרָה
מְטֹרֶפֶת עַל עַצְמָהּ, מֵאֶבֶן הַקֶּלַע וְעַל לַנַּפָּץ הַגַּרְעִינִי.
הִיא עוֹשָׂה אוֹתָנוּ וְאָנוּ עוֹשִׂים אוֹתָהּ לְלֹא תַּכְלִית... הַאִם
הַהִיסְטוֹרְיָה לֹא נוֹלְדָה כִּרְצוֹנֵנוּ, מִשּׁוּם
שֶׁהַיְצוּר הָאֱנוֹשִׁי לֹא הָיָה קַיָּם?
פִילוֹסוֹפִים וְאָמָנִים עָבְרוּ מִשָּׁם...

and the poets wrote down the dailiness of their purple flowers
then passed through there... and the poor believed
in sayings about paradise and waited there...
and gods came to rescue nature from our divinity
and passed through there. And history has no
time for contemplation, history has no mirror
and no bare face. It is unreal reality
or unfanciful fancy, so don't write it.
Don't write it, don't write it as poetry!

Translated by Dr. Foady Joudah

וְהַמְשׁוֹרְרִים רָשְׁמוּ אֶת יוֹמָנֵי הַסְּגֻלִּיּוֹת
אַחַר־כָּךְ עָבְרוּ מִשָּׁם... וְהָעֲנִיִּים הֶאֱמִינוּ
לְסִפּוּרִים עַל גַּן הָעֵדֶן וְחִכּוּ שָׁם...
וְאֵלִים בָּאוּ לְהַצִּיל אֶת הַטֶּבַע מֵאֱלֹהֵיּוּתֵנוּ
וְעָבְרוּ מִשָּׁם. וְאֵין לַהִיסְטוֹרְיָה
זְמַן לְהִתְבּוֹנְנוּת, אֵין לַהִיסְטוֹרְיָה מַרְאֶה
וּפָנִים גְּלוּיִים. הִיא מְצִיאוּת לֹא מְצִיאוּתִית
אוֹ דִמְיוֹן לֹא דִמְיוֹנִי, לָכֵן, אַל תִּכְתֹּב אוֹתָהּ
אַל תִּכְתֹּב אוֹתָהּ, אַל תִּכְתֹּב אוֹתָהּ בְּשִׁיר!

Another Day Will Come

Another day will come, a womanly day
diaphanous in metaphor, complete in being,
diamond and processional in visitation, sunny,
flexible, with a light shadow. No one will feel
a desire for suicide or leaving. All
things, outside the past, natural and real,
will be synonyms of their early traits. As if time
is slumbering on vacation... "Extend your lovely
beauty-time. Sunbathe in the sin of your silken breasts,
and wait until good omen arrives. Later
we will grow older. We have enough time
to grow older after this day..." /
Another day will come, a womanly day
songlike in gesture, lapis in getting
and in phrase. All things will be feminine outside
the past. Water will flow from rock's bosom.
No dust, no drought, no defeat.
And a dove will sleep in the afternoon in an abandoned
combat tank if it doesn't find a small nest
in the lovers' bed...

Translated by Dr. Foady Joudah

יבוא יום אחר

יָבוֹא יוֹם אַחֵר, יוֹם נָשִׁי
שָׁקוּף בְּדִמּוּי, מֻשְׁלָם בִּיצִירָה,
יוֹם כְּיַהֲלוֹם, חֲגִיגִי בְּבִיקּוּרוֹ, שִׁמְשִׁי
נוֹחַ, שֶׁצִּלּוֹ קָלִיל. אִישׁ לֹא יָחוּשׁ
בְּרָצוֹן לְהִתְאַבֵּד אוֹ לָמוּת. וְכָל
דָּבָר, מֵחוּץ לְעָבָר, יִהְיֶה טִבְעִי אֲמִתִּי,
זֵהֶה לִתְכוּנוֹתָיו הָרִאשׁוֹנִיּוֹת. כְּאִלּוּ הַזְּמַן
נָם לוֹ בְּחָפְשָׁתוֹ... "הַאֲרִיכִי אֶת עֵת נוֹיֵךְ
הַיָּפָה. הִתְחַמְּמִי בְּשֶׁמֶשׁ שְׁדֵי הַמֶּשִׁי שֶׁלָּךְ,
וְצַפִּי לַבְּשׂוֹרָה עַד שֶׁתָּבוֹא. אַחַר-כָּךְ
נִתְבַּגֵּר. יֵשׁ לָנוּ עוֹד זְמַן
לְהִתְבַּגֵּר לְאַחַר הַיּוֹם הַזֶּה..." /
יָבוֹא יוֹם אַחֵר, יוֹם נָשִׁי
שֶׁמֶּחְוָתוֹ שִׁירָה, תִּכֹּל בְּרָכָה
וּבְטוּי. כָּל דָּבָר עָנֹג מֵחוּץ
לְעָבָר. מִשַּׁד הָאֶבֶן יִזְרְמוּ מַיִם.
לֹא אָבָק, וְלֹא יֹבֶשׁ, וְלֹא אָבְדָן.
וְהַיּוֹנָה תָּנוּם אַחַר הַצָּהֳרַיִם בְּטַנְק
נָטוּשׁ אִם לֹא תִּמְצָא קֵן קָטָן
בְּמִטַּת זוּג אוֹהֲבִים...

Adi Keissar

(1981–)

Adi Keissar is a contemporary Israeli poet who has emerged as an important voice in what is termed "Mizrahi" poetry (the word *mizrahi* is often used to refer to Israelis who arrived in Israel from Arab or Muslim lands). Keissar, of Yemenite descent, refers to her poetry as *Ars Poetica*, which is both a reference to the Latin term meaning the "Art of Poetry" as well as to the Israeli slang word *ars*, taken from the Arabic word for "pimp," and often used as a derogatory term for people of a Mizrahi background. For Keissar, *Ars Poetica* constitutes a new wave of cultural creation that expresses the neglected and denigrated richness and fervor of Mizrahi culture. Her poetry, often delivered in a dynamic spoken-word performance, presents a synergy of the senses and constitutes a vibrant new voice in Israeli life.

Anatomy

Everyone always speaks of the heart.

But what about the kidneys?
Don't they know how to love?
And the liver?
Didn't all the chocolate words
that were spoken to us melt in it?
And the fingernails,
don't they bloom like flowers
when the blood says spring?
And don't the bowels hold
all the words that were hurled at us
like heavy stones?
Don't the lungs remember
the moment
they chose us
from all the people in the world?
And the navel,
doesn't it feel
how they cut the cord
and we were torn from the person
we once lived in
and now lives inside us?

Everyone always speaks of the heart.

Translated by Ayelet Tsabari

אנטומיה

כָּל הַזְּמַן מְדַבְּרִים עַל הַלֵּב.

וּמָה עִם הַכְּלָיוֹת?
הֵן לֹא יוֹדְעוֹת לֶאֱהֹב?
וְהַכָּבֵד?
לֹא נָמַסוּ בּוֹ כָּל מְלוֹת הַשּׁוֹקוֹלָד
שֶׁאָמְרוּ לָנוּ?
וְהַצִּפָּרְנַיִם, בְּאֶצְבְּעוֹת הַיָּדַיִם
לֹא צוֹמְחוֹת כְּמוֹ פְּרָחִים
כְּשֶׁהָדָם אָמַר אָבִיב?
וְהַקֵּבָה לֹא מַחְזִיקָה בְּתוֹכָהּ
אֶת כָּל הַמִּלִּים שֶׁזָּרְקוּ עָלֵינוּ
כְּמוֹ אֲבָנִים כְּבֵדוֹת?
וְהָרֵאוֹת לֹא זוֹכְרוֹת
אֶת הָרֶגַע הַהוּא
שֶׁבָּחֲרוּ בָּנוּ
בָּנוּ
מִכָּל הָאֲנָשִׁים בָּעוֹלָם?
וְהַטַּבּוּר לֹא מַרְגִּישׁ
אֵיךְ נִתְּקוּ אֶת הַחֶבֶל
וְנִשְׁמַטְנוּ מֵהָאָדָם
שֶׁפַּעַם חָיִינוּ בְּתוֹכוֹ
וְהוּא חַי בָּנוּ?

כָּל הַזְּמַן מְדַבְּרִים עַל הַלֵּב.

A Poem for Those

For those whose parents were born in the right country
and have the right surname
for those who have the right skin color
and the right eye color
for those who were born in the right city
in the right neighborhood
and went to the right school
and the right university
for those who speak the right language
in the right accent
for those who were born to the right gender
the right religion
the right nationality
the right passport
for those who were born in the right time
and have the right future

One day
when the others will come
to knock on the door
they won't be asking for a cup of sugar
they will ask
to take the door off its hinges
and tear down the house.

Translated by Ayelet Tsabari

שיר למי

לְמִי שֶׁהַהוֹרִים שֶׁלוֹ נוֹלְדוּ בַּמְּדִינָה הַנְּכוֹנָה
וְיֵשׁ לוֹ אֶת שֵׁם הַמִּשְׁפָּחָה הַנָּכוֹן
לְמִי שֶׁיֵּשׁ לוֹ אֶת צֶבַע הָעוֹר הַנָּכוֹן
וְעֵינַיִם בַּצֶּבַע הַנָּכוֹן
לְמִי שֶׁנּוֹלַד בָּעִיר הַנְּכוֹנָה
בַּשְּׁכוּנָה הַנְּכוֹנָה
וְהָלַךְ לְבֵית הַסֵּפֶר הַנָּכוֹן
וְלָאוּנִיבֶרְסִיטָה הַנְּכוֹנָה
לְמִי שֶׁמְּדַבֵּר אֶת הַשָּׂפָה הַנְּכוֹנָה
בַּמִּבְטָא הַנָּכוֹן
לְמִי שֶׁנּוֹלַד לַמִּין הַנָּכוֹן
לַדָּת הַנְּכוֹנָה
לַלְּאֹם הַנָּכוֹן
לַדֵּרְכוֹן הַנָּכוֹן
לְמִי שֶׁנּוֹלַד בַּזְּמַן הַנָּכוֹן
וְיֵשׁ לוֹ אֶת הֶעָתִיד הַנָּכוֹן

יוֹם אֶחָד
כְּשֶׁהֵם יָבוֹאוּ
לִדְפֹּק בַּדֶּלֶת
הֵם לֹא יְבַקְשׁוּ כּוֹס סֻכָּר
הֵם יְבַקְשׁוּ
לַעֲקֹר אֶת הַדֶּלֶת מִמְּקוֹמָהּ
וּלְמוֹטֵט אֶת הַבַּיִת.

GRATEFUL ACKNOWLEDGMENT IS MADE FOR PERMISSION TO REPRINT THE FOLLOWING PREVIOUSLY PUBLISHED WORKS:

NATHAN ALTERMAN: "The Silver Platter," and "Song of the Homeland," reproduced from *The Zionist Ideas: Visions for the Jewish Homeland — Then, Now, Tomorrow*, edited by Gil Troy, with permission of the University of Nebraska Press. ©2018 by Gil Troy. Poems ©ACUM.

YEHUDA AMICHAI: "And the Child is No More," from *The Poetry of Yehuda Amichai* by Yehuda Amichai, edited by Robert Alter. ©2015 by Hana Amichai. Introduction and selection copyright ©2015 by Robert Alter. Translation reprinted by permission of Farrar, Straus and Giroux. "Instead of a love poem," "Tourists," and "Jerusalem," ©Schocken Publishing House Ltd., Tel Aviv, Israel and ©Hana Amichai.

HAIM NACHMAN BIALIK: "At the Window She Sits," from "To the Bird," and from "In The City of Slaughter." Translations reprinted, with the permission of David Aberbach ©David Aberbach.

EREZ BITON: "A Purchase on Dizengov," and "Yom Kippur at the School for the Blind" from *You Who Crossed My Path: Selected Poems*, translated by Tsipi Keller (Rochester: BOA Editions, 2015), 98, 176. ©2015 BOA Editions, with permission from BOA Editions.

RACHEL BLUWSTEIN: Translations of "Was it only a dream..." and "Love Was Late in Coming" reprinted with permission from Jean Shapiro Cantu ©Jean Shapiro Cantu for the Estate of Robert Friend.

ELIAZ COHEN: "Hear O God (Hear, O Lord)," and "Selection from With Me From Lebanon." Poems and translations reprinted with permission from Eliaz Cohen ©Eliaz Cohen.

MAHMOUD DARWISH: "Another Day Will Come," "This is Forgetfulness," and "Don't Write History as Poetry" from the *Butterfly's Burden*, translated into English by Dr. Fady Joudah ©2007 Mahmoud Darwish, translation ©2007 by Dr. Fady Joudah. Reprinted with permission of The Permissions Company, LLC on behalf of Copper Canyon Press, coppercanyonpress.org. "Another Day Will Come," "This is Forgetfulness," and "Don't Write History as Poetry," translated into Hebrew by Ehud Horowitz reprinted with permission ©Keshev Leshira.

LEA GOLDBERG: "Tel Aviv 1935," "A God Once Commanded Us," and "Toward Myself," reprinted with permission from Hakibbutz Hameuchad - Sifriat Poalim, all rights of Lea Goldberg's poems belong to Hakibbutz Hameuchad - Sifriat Poalim. Translations reprinted with permission from Jean Shapiro Cantu ©Jean Shapiro Cantu for the Estate of Robert Friend.

CHAIM GURI: "Bab El Wad," translation reprinted with the permission of Vivian Eden ©Vivian Eden and "Inheritance," reprinted from *Words in my Lovesick Blood* by Haim Gouri [sic.], translated by Stanley Chyet ©1996 Wayne State University Press, with the permission of Wayne State University Press. All Chaim Guri poems ©ACUM.

ACKNOWLEDGMENTS

This book would never have happened without the minds, passion, and efficiency of Erika Vogel and Natalie Blitt, who guided this volume from inception to completion. Special thanks to Anne Lanski, Director of The iCenter for Israel Education who provided the oversight and leadership for this project and who championed the educational value of this resource from the beginning.

Our gratitude to Mitch Ginsburg for his innovative and creative eye as an editor and to Nadia Jacobson for her astute copy-editing skills. To Ari Feinstein, Ayal Weiner-Kaplow, Jessica Lewis, and countless other members of The iCenter team, thank you for the endless hours spent proofreading, hunting down translations, and ensuring the accuracy of our citations. Our appreciation to Michal Peles-Almagor for her assistance in adding the missing nikkud, tracking down hard to find Hebrew poems, and assisting in securing permissions, along with other integral tasks.

Warm thanks to our designers Kristy Scher and Meredith Swartz who worked tirelessly on creating the perfect cover and layout for this anthology, and to Shira Stav for the use of her beautiful photograph that graces the book's cover.

We appreciate the assistance of Deborah Harris and Jessica Kasmer-Jacobs at important moments. Special thanks to Hana Amichai, David Aberbach, and David Greenberg. We are incredibly grateful to the poets, translators, and publishing houses for their assistance and cooperation in granting us the rights to reprint these important works. We would like to especially thank the Permission Company, LLC and ACUM for their assistance in securing the majority of the reproduction rights.

For the translation of biblical sources, we used the newly published *The Hebrew Bible: Translation with Commentary* (New York: W.W. Norton and Company, 2019) by Robert Alter whose unprecedented achievement is noteworthy.

Last, but certainly not least, our greatest thanks go to the 24 figures whose words, ideas, thinking, and selves are in this book. Each are unique individuals who together weave a rich and diverse tapestry of word and ideas. *Todah rabah!*

ABOUT THE EDITORS

Barry Chazan Barry Chazan is Professor Emeritus of the Hebrew University of Jerusalem and currently teaches at The George Washington University Graduate School of Education and Human Development.

Shai Chazan received undergraduate and graduate degrees from the Hebrew University and is Website/Communications Manager at the National Library of Israel in Jerusalem. He has served as editor and translator at the Carmel Publishing House in Jerusalem.

Yehudit Werchow received a BA in Political Science and Latin American studies from the Hebrew University of Jerusalem, an MA in in Jewish Education from Hebrew Union College-Jewish Institute of Religion New York, and rabbinical ordination from HUC-JIR in Jerusalem. She has served as Director of the Masa Israel Journeys Program and is a member of the staff of The iCenter for Israel Education.